MINIATURE RAILWAY LOCOMOTIVES AND ROLLING STOCK

Royston Morris

AMBERLEY

First published 2018

Amberley Publishing
The Hill, Stroud
Gloucestershire, GL5 4EP

www.amberley-books.com

Copyright © Royston Morris, 2018

The right of Royston Morris to be identified
as the Author of this work has been asserted
in accordance with the Copyright, Designs and
Patents Act 1988.

ISBN 978 1 4456 7791 0 (print)
ISBN 978 1 4456 7792 7 (ebook)

British Library Cataloguing in Publication Data.
A catalogue record for this book is available from
the British Library.

Origination by Amberley Publishing.
Printed in the UK.

Introduction

Following the introduction of railway locomotives to the country by Robert Stephenson in the early 1820s, several people began to build models of locomotives to either show how the finished engine would look when constructed, or so that they could see the locomotive in a much smaller scale than the original. Many of these models were also 'sectioned' to show the internal workings of the locomotive and were used as training aides in engineering schools and colleges. Several of these non-working models can be seen in museums up and down the country – usually in glass cases.

One of those modellers was Sir Arthur Percival Heywood, and he believed that railways with a gauge as small as 15 inches could be useful in carrying out jobs on private estates and in businesses alike. So in 1875, he built his first locomotive and railway at his house in Duffield, Derbyshire. He also published a book called *Minimum Gauge Railways,* and following its publication in 1896 the Duke of Westminster commissioned Heywood to build a 15 inch gauge railway on his private Eaton Hall estate in Cheshire. It still survives to this day and has occasional open days to the public.

Towards the end of the nineteenth century, the Cagney brothers from America came up with the idea of running small railways as tourist pleasure attractions, and sought to bring some of their locomotives to this country. This led to a partnership between astute businessman W. J. Bassett-Lowke and designer Henry Greenly, whereupon they decided that they were going to build small railway locomotives, which in 1905, at Bassett-Lowke's works in Northampton, produced a 15 inch gauge locomotive named *Little Giant.* The company was soon then supplying railway equipment in 7¼ inch, 9½ inch and 15 inch gauges, often to the customer's own specifications – ranging from castings and drawings to fully completed railways (including locomotives and carriages). However, the 9½ inch gauge proved not to be as popular as the other gauges and by 1910 it was replaced by the 10¼ inch gauge, and Bassett-Lowke continued selling right up until 1939. Thus it was that the miniature railway scene came into existence in the UK.

After the war, for the next thirty odd years, miniature railways enjoyed their busiest and most prosperous times, and saw a boom in the increase of these types of attractions right up until the mid-1980s, when things began to slow down. During the late 1980s and early 1990s, due to the change in trend where people wanted their leisure attractions to offer more adrenaline-pumping rides (such as those offered at places like Thorpe Park and Alton Towers, etc.), many miniature railways suffered a low, with turnouts dropping and some lines being closed forever – although, thankfully, there were a significant number that kept going. In more recent years, however, the miniature railway scene has experienced an upturn in its fortunes again – with new locomotives, lines and attractions still being built. These attractions delight children and adults alike and many of these railways are hired out for birthday parties, weddings and other special family occasions.

Although I have been interested in railways since the mid-1970s, my interest in miniature railways has really taken off following a visit in June 2006 to the Moors Valley Country Park in Ashley Heath, near Ringwood in Hampshire, where they had around twenty miniature locomotives running through the park on an intensive 7¼ inch gauge layout. Until that moment I had regarded miniature railways as kiddies' trains – how wrong I was about that. I try to visit as many miniature railway attractions as possible nowadays because they are fascinating, with some quite diverse locomotives, as well as the ones that are scaled-down replicas of main line locomotives.

However, I have included pictures of these locomotives because I feel you cannot do a book on miniature railways and not include them. After all, if it wasn't for people like Sir Arthur and Messrs Bassett-Lowke and Greenly, then we wouldn't have a miniature railway scene in this country on the scale that we do today.

The photographs in this book were all taken by myself from 2005 right up to the present day and they contain locomotives of all gauges between 3½ inch and 15 inch, as well as coaches and freight stock. I hope you enjoy this book as much as I've enjoyed compiling it.

Chapter 1 – The Basics

There are two types of railways that are referred to as non-main line or non-standard gauge. These are rideable miniature railways and narrow gauge or minimum gauge railways. I shall try to explain the differences between the two.

Rideable miniature railways are basically pleasure lines that operate on all gauges between 3½ inches and 15 inches. These can be found carrying fare-paying passengers at locations where the railways are permanently sited, be that either designated and recognised sites or club/society tracks, or they can be found at temporary locations on what are known as portable railways.

Narrow gauge or minimum gauge railways were originally designed to carry out work on estates, or in coal mines and steel works, for example. They cover all gauges from 15 inches up to 4 feet. They are usually working industrial locomotives that do not carry passengers, although several of these locomotives have been preserved and often see regular passenger use on preservation lines throughout the country.

The coaching stock used on rideable miniature railways can be divided up into three categories: the 'ride-on' or 'sit-astride' type; the 'sit-in' open type; and the 'ride-in' enclosed type. These will be explained in the captions under the photographs. Many freight wagons are also used; some where the driver sits and some that are occasionally used for people to take photographs of a freight special, but where no passengers are normally carried. Others are also built for use on track maintenance, and so on.

For means of ease I have listed the locations in alphabetical order for all gauges covered within this book and I have also included their location, post code and website (where applicable) in order that this may be of some assistance to any reader who wishes to visit some of these fascinating railways.

All the photographs in this book are of the rideable miniature railways type.

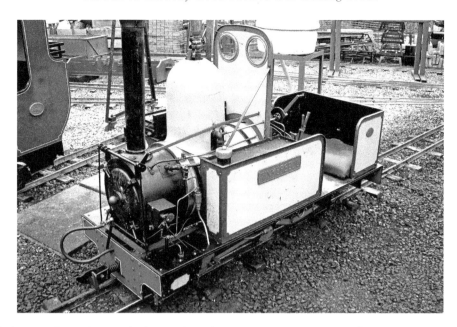

The Moors Valley Railway was built in 1985/86 and runs on an extensive 1.75 miles of track within the grounds of the Moors Valley Country Park in Ashley Heath, near Ringwood, Hampshire, BH24 2ET. The railway has about seventeen steam locomotives and two diesels, which guarantees that they are one of the few miniature railways that runs steam every day that are open throughout the year. Here is the locomotive that started it all, No. 4 *Tinkerbell,* which is a 0-4-2T engine. It was built in 1968 by Roger Marsh and was purchased by the owner of the Moors Valley, Jim Haylock, in 1978. It is seen taking on water prior to starting working on passenger trains on 24 March 2013.

Pictured at the Direct Rail Services Limited public open day at their Kingmoor depot in Carlisle is this 5 inch gauge carriage, which is sporting, appropriately enough, DRS livery. This type of carriage is known as a 'ride-on' or 'sit-astride', and is self-explanatory by nature, insomuch that you sit on it with your legs on either side and your feet on the boards along the bottom of the carriage. This type of line is only temporary and the setback with carriages of this gauge that are at ground level is that, invariably, the passengers' knees are almost hitting them in the face due to the uncomfortable position they are in. The picture was taken on 18 July 2015.

Among the few vehicles that work on the privately owned and run 10¼ inch gauge Highland Light Railway, at the Mill of Logierait Farm near Ballinluig in Scotland, are the two wagons featured in this picture. The one on the right is a three-planked open wagon, which is used to carry farm produce from the fields to the storage barns that are located alongside the 1,380-yard-long railway, and the one nearest the camera is a permanent way wagon (No. 10) that has been fitted with a Hiab-type lifting device that can lift track or sleepers and can operate at a 90 degree angle to either side of the wagon. It also has a couple of halogen spotlights for use in failing light. Note the four stabilisers fitted to each corner, which are lowered onto the ballast when the crane is in use. The picture was taken on 25 March 2016.

Chapter 2 – 3½ Inch Gauge

Locomotives built to this gauge are more often than not only seen on some 'club tracks', which are mainly for their members to run their locomotives on if they wish. However, locomotives and track of this gauge are extremely rare nowadays. There are a few locations that run dual-gauge tracks of 3½ inch gauge and 5 inch gauge, but not many, with most locations choosing the 5 inch gauge as their smallest on which to run trains with.

This locomotive was built in 1911 by James Carson, and is a scaled-down version of the Great Western Railway's 4-6-2 Pacific No. 111 *The Great Bear*. It ran for many years in the owner's garden on his privately owned railway. It can be seen nowadays, however, as a static model at the Sir William McAlpine Fawley Hill Railway & Museum in Buckinghamshire, which has occasional public open running days. The photograph was taken on one such day on 3 June 2012.

Another former working locomotive of this gauge, which also now sees out its days at the Fawley Hill Railway & Museum on display as a model, is this 2-8-0, modelled on the Great Western Railway 7F 47xx Class. Here, No. 4702 was also photographed on 3 June 2012.

Completing this trio of 3½ inch gauge former working locomotives is No. 6002 *King William IV*, which is a scaled-down version of a Great Western Railway 4-6-0 6oxx King Class passenger locomotive. This was also photographed at Fawley Hill Railway & Museum on 3 June 2012. Note the wagons in between the two locomotives; these are also of 3½ inch gauge.

Chapter 3 – 5 Inch Gauge

A good number of 'club tracks' use this gauge and the 7¼ inch gauge on one dual track. The track consists of three rails (giving them the appearance of the third rail, as seen on London Underground for example). The distance between the two outer rails is 7¼ inches and the distance between the one on the left-hand side, in the direction of travel, and the third inner rail is 5 inches. The biggest part of these types of track are found at a raised or elevated level only in order to be able to accommodate the passenger carriages. Where a dual-gauge track is found at ground level, this saves the club money by not having to lay two separate sets of tracks. I should explain here that the term 'club track' is usually given to a club or society (Society of Model Engineers, etc.) that has its own location where they hold meetings for their members and where locomotives and stock are not normally kept, but are brought there by the owners on running days. The majority of these are not normally regularly open to the public, but they might operate on the first Sunday of the month, for example, or they might hold occasional public open running days.

These gauge locomotives can sometimes be found operating on short lengths of track at steam rallies and vintage/classic car shows in the form of portable railways.

Photographed on 22 August 2009, at the North London Society of Model Engineers at Colney Heath, was this beautiful-looking working model of the London & North Eastern 4-4-0 locomotive No. 1306 *Mayflower*. The main reason for it being so immaculately clean was that the owner had only finished overhauling it a couple of days beforehand, and that day was its first public running for a couple of years.

The water works at Twyford in Hampshire has a 2 foot narrow gauge railway that runs around inside its complex and they hold occasional open days during the year. On the final running day on 2 October 2011, members of the Winchester Model & Engineering Society were giving rides on a short section of raised track (100 yards) behind one of their 5 inch gauge steam locomotives. This one, *Bunny*, is closely modelled on a Southern Railway Class E2 0-6-0T locomotive, but is not quite an exact replica. Due to the track being raised off the ground, the sit-astride coaches dwarf the locomotive, but allow for the passengers to be sat in a more comfortable position than they would be if the track was at ground level.

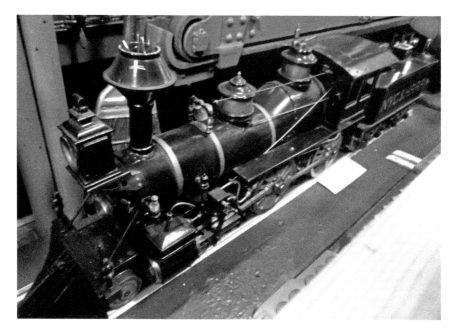

One of the interesting things I find about miniature railways is the variety of locomotives that can be found on a visit to one of these lines (as well as at some standard gauge heritage railways throughout the country). For instance, on display beside a standard gauge freight wagon at the Mangapps Farm Railway Museum in Burnham-on-Crouch in Essex on 15 June 2013 was this 5 inch gauge 2-6-0 steam locomotive, modelled on an American locomotive from the New York Central & Hudson River Railroad (which ran between 1869 and 1914).

On display inside the model tent at the Launceston Steam & Vintage Rally on 24 May 2015 was this working steam locomotive, which was built by a local gentleman from the area. This 0-4-0, named *Polly II*, is used in the owner's back garden and at his local club track. The angle from which I took the photograph gives the engine the appearance of being much larger than the 5 inch gauge it is – even the track looks enormous!

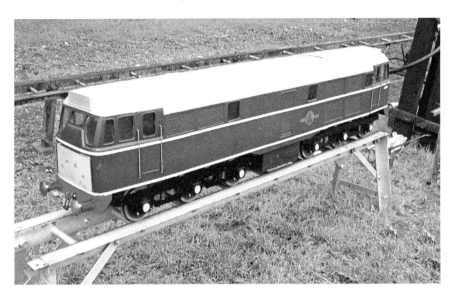

Pictured at the open day of the Claude Jessett Trust in Hadlow Down on 4 August 2012 was this Brush Type 2-modelled Class 31 A1A-A1A locomotive, which was numbered D5512, and is seen while resting between giving rides. Note the metal tressle frame; this is collapsible and can be removed from site, and is used to load/unload locomotives at locations.

The English Electric Type 3 Class 37 Co-Co locomotive is one of the most popular diesel locomotives that have ever been built, so it is hardly surprising that model engineers should build scale models of them. This example, No. 37408 *Linda* (named after the builder's wife), was built by a member of the Taunton Model & Engineering Society and is a 5 inch gauge battery-electric version. It is seen looking resplendent in its EWS red and yellow livery as it poses between giving rides to the public at the Steam on the Levels event at Westonzoyland Pumping Station on the Somerset Levels on 15 May 2016. Note the amount of wires leading from the engine to the operator's control box, seen nearest the camera.

Sadly none of the ten English Electric Napier Class 23 Baby Deltic locomotives that were built in 1959 survived to go on to preservation. That doesn't stop model engineers from replicating them, however. Here, D5908 waits for passengers as it prepares to gives rides to the public at the East Kent Light Railway in Shepherdswell on 19 April 2014. Note the missing buffer and headcode panel from the nose of the locomotive; although, as the majority of people who ride these trains are predominantly children, I'm fairly certain that none of them would have noticed.

The Direct Rail Services open day held at the company's Carlisle depot on 18 July 2015 saw a short section of 5 inch gauge track at ground level giving rides. Among the locomotives and stock being used was this model of one of the 50T Bogie Nuclear Flask Carrying Wagons. This can be placed behind the locomotive and the driver would sit on the centre (flask) part to operate the train while giving rides. Note the DRS-liveried Class 66 locomotive on the table behind the wagon. The nose of a DRS-liveried Class 20 can just be seen on the right of the picture as well. Both of these locomotives were used throughout the day, along with a DRS-liveried Class 37.

Chapter 4 – 7¼ Inch Gauge

This is the most popular miniature railway gauge that has ever been used in this country, and therefore invariably represents the majority of the content within this book.

The majority of locations throughout use this gauge and some have extensive layouts with several locomotives being regularly used and based there. Some examples include the Mizens Railway in Woking, the Great Cockrow Railway near Chertsey, the Beer Heights Light Railway in Beer, Devon, the Moors Valley Country Park near Ringwood and the Bentley Wildfowl Park in Halland.

These locations are normally open to the public at any time between Easter and October – some at weekends and all day during school holidays, others just at weekends and Bank Holidays. If you are thinking about visiting one of the many miniature railways that can be found in the UK, I would advise you try looking at their website (note not all locations do have a website) or ringing them to find out their opening days and times.

As you will see from the photographs, although all of these locomotives are the same gauge, the various sizes in scales are abundantly obvious. The popularity of this gauge is clearly noted, as when the 7¼ Inch Gauge Society hold their annual AGM (which is usually at one of the railways in the UK), they can have up to 100 of their members' locomotives on display, and many of them running.

Adjacent to the Audley End Miniature Railway in Saffron Walden, Essex, is a triple-gauge (3½ inch, 5 inch and 7¼ inch) elevated and ground level set of tracks, which is operated by members of the Saffron Walden & District Society of Model Engineers. One of their locomotives is this four-wheel petrol-hydraulic, No. 5 *Doris,* built by member J. Dickinson in 2008. It is seen here in between passenger duties on Easter Monday 21 April 2014. Details of the society can be found at www.swdsme.org.uk.

Located at post code DY3 4HB in Dudley, West Midlands, is the Baggeridge Country Park, and within the park is the railway that is operated by the Wolverhampton & District Model Engineering Society. In 2005 the society members built this 4w-4w petrol-hydraulic locomotive, No. 20 *Baggeridge Ranger*, which I photographed after it had run the last passenger working for the day on 29 July 2012. Note the elevated dual-gauge 3½ inch and 5 inch track in the background that runs alongside the 7¼ inch gauge line. Details can be found at www.wolverhampton-dmes.co.uk.

Bankside Miniature Railway is located within the site of the Brambridge Park Garden Centre near Winchester in Hampshire, SO50 6HT. It is quite unusual as it has an elevated track of 8¼ inch gauge and a ground level track of 7¼ inch gauge. The railway has two locomotives of the latter gauge and one of the former gauge. On 12 October 2013 this 1994-built 7¼ inch gauge 0-6-0ST, No. 2130, was running trains for the public. Note that the driver sits on top of the round black water tank in order to operate it (the tank can be seen behind the locomotive).

In 1989 a new railway opened at the Barleylands Visitor Centre in Billericay, Essex, CM11 2UD, and is known as the Barleylands Miniature Railway. The majority of the track, locomotives and stock all came from the closed North Benfleet Miniature Railway, which used to operate in the town near Basildon. The railway has six locomotives, comprising five steam engines and a petrol-hydraulic. At the time of my visit on Easter Monday 21 April 2014, the five steam locomotives were all out of service and in various stages of undergoing overhauls. The Roanoke Engineering-built PH locomotive, named *Dereck* (note the unusual spelling of name), was being used on passenger services, and is seen here ready to depart with a train full of passengers on a sunny afternoon. Worth noting is the large headlight on the front of the locomotive, which is a common feature on locomotives built by this company. Details of running days can be found at www.barleylands.co.uk.

On 11 October 2014 the 7¼ Inch Gauge Society held its Annual General Meeting (AGM) at the Bath & West Railway, where there were in excess of fifty plus visiting locomotives in attendance. This event is usually held at a different railway in the country each year. It encourages the owners to drive their locomotives around on these public-operated railways, as many owners either only drive them on lines placed in their gardens or on 'club-tracks', meaning the locos hardly ever get used to their fullest capacity. This event gives them the chance to do so. Throughout the day the majority of the trains are single engines, although some owners do decide to double-head their engines. One such occasion saw the pairing of these two immaculate steam locomotives, headed by 2-4-2+T No. 1 *Afon Glaslyn* and 2-4-2 No. 2 *Tarn Beck* as they set off along the first stretch of straight line shortly after leaving the station site with its curves and crossovers. The railway runs both steam and diesel trains (on days when events are taking place) on the line that was built and operated by volunteers of the East Somerset Society of Model & Experimental Engineers, which was founded in 2001 (www.essmee.org.uk). The railway is located within the site of the Royal Bath & West Showground just outside Shepton Mallet in Somerset, BA4 6QN.

On 14 July 1975 the Reverend Wilbert Vere Awdry (author of the children's book series *Thomas the Tank Engine*) opened a brand-new 7¼ inch gauge miniature railway, which was to prove to be a popular tourist attraction in Beer, Devon. It operates on a site adjacent to the Pecorama Pleasure Gardens, EX12 3NA, which is owned by the UK-based company Peco, who manufacture (on the same site) model railway accessories. This new railway was known as the Beer Heights Light Railway, which has grown since its inception over forty years ago and operates a very extensive layout spread out for just over a mile. The railway is home to eight or nine steam locomotives and a couple of diesel/battery-electric locomotives. The railway's chief mechanical engineer, John Macdougall (pictured in bowler hat), designed and built the brand new petrol-engined locomotive *Ben* (named by BBC News Correspondent Ben Ando). This 4w-4w locomotive made its inaugural run during the railway's 40th anniversary celebrations and is pictured here just starting that run on 30 August 2015. You can find out more about this fantastic railway at www.pecorama.co.uk.

The railway's 40th anniversary celebrations on 30 August 2015 saw the railway operate a unique and certainly never to be repeated event. This took the form of a quadruple-headed train with all four locomotives in steam, and it is seen here arriving back at Much Natter station. The train was headed by resident 1979-built 0-4-2 engine No. 4 *Thomas II*, with visiting locomotives the 2007-built 2-4-2+T No. 2 *Afon Glaslyn*, an unnumbered 2011-built 2-4-0ST, followed at the rear by another resident locomotive, the 2004-built 2-4-2 No. 1 *Otter*.

Bekonscot Model Village in Beaconsfield, Buckinghamshire, HP9 2PL, is also home to the Bekonscot Light Railway, where their own 2001-built 4w-4w battery-electric railcar, No. 3, was photographed parked up and not in service on 12 August 2017. The railcar was made by converting a 'sit-astride' open coach: widening the bottom foot step sides, adding a roof, motors, controls and brake levers on both ends. The railway winds its way around about 200 yards of track complete with a figure of eight crossover at its upper end, where part of the model village can be observed. Further information, including opening times, can be found at www.bekonscot.co.uk.

One of the fascinating things that I find with miniature railways is the variety of locomotives that can be seen and the degree of differences in sizes of these locomotives, as shown in this picture, taken at the Bentley Miniature Railway on 3 August 2012. It shows two 0-4-0 petrol locomotives; on the left is a *c.* 1996-built petrol-hydraulic locomotive named *Rachel*, with 2012-built petrol-electric locomotive No. 2957 alongside. Despite the fact that these both of these locomotives are of 7¼ inch gauge, and therefore run on the same track, the different sizes in scale used by the builders are clearly evident. This is usually due to the fact that they are built by different people/societies/clubs; if you have any two locomotives (which are by the same builder) they are normally both built to the same scale, and therefore there are no noticeable differences in sizes. You might occasionally find a locomotive with difference in size scales from the same builder, but these are quite rare.

Despite being a model engineers-based club track, this railway is unique in that several of the locomotives that run here are actually kept on site. The dual-gauge (5 inch and 7¼ inch) 1-mile-long track is situated within the grounds of the Bentley Wildfowl Park and Motor Museum in Halland, East Sussex, BN8 5AF (www. bentleyrailway.co.uk). The railway is run by members of the Uckfield Model Railway Club, who have built a number of the locomotives that are based here. One of the more unusual of these is this permanently coupled five-car battery-electric railcar named *Bentley Belle* from 2009, which was photographed in the early morning sunshine on 3 August 2012. Due to the length of this vehicle, the members of the club have built its own shed, which is used purposely to house the locomotive.

Brookside Garden Centre in Poynton, Cheshire, SK12 1BY, is where you will find the Brookside Miniature Railway, which winds its way through the very busy garden centre with a small fleet of locomotives. Photographed preparing to depart with a train full of passengers on 15 August 2015 is one of the five steam locomotives that the railway has on site. This example is No. 314 *Amy Louise,* a 0-4-2T type that was built in 2003. All of the railway's steam locomotives were built in North Devon by the Exmoor Steam Railway. More information can be found at www.brooksideminiaturerailway.co.uk.

In 1962 a model engineering society known as the Hereford Live Steamers was formed. They eventually changed their name to Hereford Society of Model Engineers due to them not only concentrating on steam locomotives (as they did when they were formed, as steam locomotives were still the major type of motive power on Britain's railways at that time). The society operates the Broomy Hill Railway, which is allocated adjacent to the Waterworks in Hereford, HR4 0LJ, and their running times at this club track can be found at www.hsme.co.uk. On 30 September 2007 this 0-4-2 locomotive, named *Leviathan*, which was built in 2003, was photographed being filled up with water ahead of running trains for the day.

Conwy Valley Railway opened in 1979 within the site of the Conwy Valley Railway Museum in Betws-y-Coed, Conwy, LL24 0AL. The museum has many interesting things to see, including a standard gauge Pullman railway carriage, a 15 inch gauge railway and also a 7¼ inch gauge railway (see www.conwyrailwaymuseum.co.uk for further details). 6 April 2007 saw this 2004-built 2-4-0T locomotive, *Dragonfly*, posing for the camera, giving a great side profile of the engine as it stands in front of the Pullman carriage previously mentioned. By August 2014 this locomotive was noted at its new home on the Dragon Miniature Railway in Marple.

The Taunton Model Engineers Society until recently ran two miniature railways – an elevated dual-gauge 3½ inch and 5 inch gauge track within Vivary Park in Taunton, TA1 3SX, and a dual-gauge 5 inch and 7¼ inch gauge ground level track at Creech St Michael, Somerset. Sadly, and much to the chagrin and annoyance of a great number of people who live in the village of Creech St Michael, during the spring of 2017 the Creech Parish Council gave the railway notice to quit its site (which was located in the recreation ground), and therefore this highly popular and well used railway was forced to close. At the time of writing the society is looking to try and relocate to another permanent site, but with not much success so far. Pictured in happier days at the Creech Miniature Railway, during a gala day on 23 July 2016, were three trains, fully loaded with passengers, as was usual at this railway. Nearest the camera is a 2-8-0 locomotive, No. 4701. Behind that is an unnumbered 0-4-0T locomotive and bringing up the rear is a 4-4-0 locomotive, No. 1096. Hopefully the society can find a new permanent home somewhere locally, where people of all ages can once again enjoy riding on the trains.

A vast number of miniature railways tend to thrive when they are based at locations where there are numerous other attractions, and not all of them railway related either. One of these many such railways is the Cultra Light Railway, where the Model Engineers Society of Northern Ireland run a dual-gauge elevated track of 3½ inch and 5 inch and a ground level 7¼ inch line. The railway is located within the grounds of the popular Ulster Folk & Transport Museum in Cultra, County Down, BT18 0EU (www.nmni.com/uftm). Pictured at this location on 4 April 2015 at the end of the day's running were the members-built 0-6-0 locomotive of 1999, *Lady Grange* (nearest the camera), and the 2010-built 0-4-0 locomotive *Jean Anderson*.

The Donegal Railway Heritage Centre, located at the Old Station House in Donegal Town in the Republic of Ireland, is home to a very interesting railway museum and some old Donegal Railway carriages, and ran until 2011 a short length of 7¼ inch gauge line along the rear of the former platform. Pictured on 29 April 2011 was this Ruston-based 4w battery-electric locomotive, which was built by Maxitrak Ltd and was numbered 628. The line out of sight, about 20 feet behind me, had been severely damaged due to flooding that had occurred following a recent storm, and the track and part of the former platform had been devastated. The heritage centre still has the locomotive, which was found locked away in a secure building when I visited again in April 2015, and they are hopeful of restoring the line in a different position on the site. More information can be found at www.donegalrailway.com.

The Dragon Miniature Railway can be found within the grounds of the Garden Centre in Dooley Lane, Marple in Greater Manchester, SK6 7HE. It is operated whenever the garden centre is open by Brian Lomas and a team of dedicated volunteers. The railway has a dozen locomotives, which are divided by 6/7 steam and 5/6 petrol-hydraulic locomotives. The railway's newest locomotive at the time of my visit on 9 August 2014 was this Brian Lomas-built 6-6w petrol-hydraulic locomotive of 2010. It is numbered D8608 and it represents the Beyer-Peacock-built Class 17 Clayton diesel-electric British Railways locomotives, of which there is only one example preserved out of the 117 built between 1962 and 1965.

One of the more unusual things seen at the railway on 9 August 2014, and something that I have never seen at any other miniature railway, is this Stuart Cameron-built 2013 representation of a British Railways standard independent snowplough. It is numbered DB965309 and is named *Snow Queen*. Incidentally, its full-size standard gauge counterpart, on which this one was modelled, was numbered DB965308 and named *Snow King*.

Built in 2005, this 7¼ inch gauge 4w-4w battery-electric locomotive was based on a Northern Ireland Railways Class 101 Bo-Bo diesel-electric. It is seen here about to enter the station at Donaghadee on the Drumawhey Junction Railway in Ireland on Easter Sunday, 5 April 2015. The extensive and complex railway is operated by members of the Belfast & County Down Miniature Railway Society, whose website is www.bcdmrs.org.uk, and who are located at Upper Gransha Road in Donaghadee, County Down, BT21 0LZ.

The railway uses the open 'sit-in' style of carriages, and this example, numbered 811 and branded with the Northern Ireland Railways logo, is different from others of its type in that it couples next to the locomotive and has a seat in the front where the driver sits. Most carriages of this type have the open two compartments with seats facing each other. It was also pictured on 5 April 2015, having arrived at Donaghadee station and its passengers having disembarked.

Several miniature railways welcome not only the members of the public but members of other societies and organisations who are not only interested in riding the trains but in other aspects of the railway as well, with many of them granting access to sheds and other areas not usually open to the general public, providing that these visits have been pre-arranged. In my role as Events Officer of the Cardiff & Avonside Railway Society, I often have the opportunity to contact these railways, where a full 'behind the scenes' visit can be arranged, as was the case on the Drumawhey Junction Railway. Pictured in one of the sheds on 5 April 2015 was this open coal wagon, which now carries a mobile generator that is used when track maintenance is carried out, usually during the closed season.

In the West Sussex countryside is a country park, which includes the 5-acre Southbourne Lake. It is here that you will find the Eastbourne Miniature Steam Railway, where you can enjoy a ride of just under a mile on the 7¼ inch railway as it meanders its way through the park, pulled by 1/8th scale models of full-size locomotives. The railway is home to about eight or nine steam locomotives and two or three petrol/battery-electric locomotives. Photographed basking in the summer sun on 3 August 2012 is this 1987 LMS-modelled 4-6-0 locomotive, No. 6172 *Royal Green Jackets*.

As well as the 1/8th scale models of locomotives, the 'sit-astride' carriages are also 1/8th scaled-down models of original coaches (as can be seen behind the steam loco). Pictured here waiting for their drivers on 3 August 2012 are replica models of an English Electric Type 3 Class 37 locomotive, D6700 *Eleventh Duke of Devonshire* (nearest the camera), which was built in 2004 and is a 6w-6w petrol-electric, and a replica Southern Railways 4-4-0 of 1998 behind it, numbered 914 and named *Eastbourne*. The railway is located at post code BN23 6QJ, and further information can be found at www.emsr.co.uk.

Harvesters station is the main three-platform station on the Echills Wood Railway, which is a 1,500-yard-long track that runs around the Kingsbury Water Park in Warwickshire, B76 0DY. The line features bridges, tunnels and a large locomotive depot (see www.ewr.org.uk for further details and information). Pictured soaking up the sun as it waits to leave the above mentioned station on 16 August 2013 is the railway's 1989-built 4w-4w diesel-hydraulic locomotive, DH1 *River Cole*, which has been painted to replicate the two-tone green livery that was carried on numerous locomotives during the 1960s and early 1970s.

The Fancott Arms Public House, near Toddington in Bedfordshire, LU5 6HT, is unique in that it is host to the oldest pub railway in England. 1975 saw a 10¼ inch line operating within the pub grounds, which was known as the Fancott Light Railway, but this line closed in 1986. Ten years later the line re-opened, this time as a 0.75-mile, 7¼ inch gauge railway. The railway was forced to close when, in the early hours of 3 March 2015, a fire destroyed some pub outbuildings, including the shed containing the locomotives and carriages. This was not the end of the railway, however, as by July of that year it had re-opened again. One of the locomotives that was serious devastated by the fire was local celebrity and pub stalwart *Herbie*. The locomotive was built in 1984 by Severn Lamb Ltd and was originally used on the Southill Light Railway, which operated at the White Horse Public House in Southill, and it came to Fancott in 1999. Following the fire it was sent to RVM Engineering in Hampshire in 2016, where it was rebuilt and returned to Fancott in March 2017. On 27 May 2017 the locomotive was re-dedicated and had its public unveiling in a ceremony that was performed in front of the local media. The special guest for the ceremony was author, *Railway Magazine* correspondent and very good friend of mine Peter Nicholson. On 10 June 2017 I visited and took this picture of *Herbie* relishing the sunshine accompanied by 0-6-0 petrol-hydraulic 2006-built locomotive No. 3 *The Phoenix*. For more information on this fascinating railway visit www.fancottrailway.co.uk.

Members of the Vale of Aylesbury Model Engineering Society (www.vames.co.uk) can run their locomotives around on the 1 kilometre of dual-gauge track (5 inch and 7¼ inch) that is located within the Buckinghamshire Railway Centre in Quainton, HP22 4BY, and which is known as the Golding Spring Miniature Railway. On 15 August 2010, 2-8-0 locomotive No. 9 *Nutty*, built by M. Hutt in 2009, emerges from the short tunnel on the railway with a train full of passengers. The dual gauge of the track can clearly be seen in front of the locomotive; note how this track has four rails (two for each gauge), as opposed to three found elsewhere.

The Great Cockrow Railway in Lyne, near Chertsey, Surrey, KT16 0AD, is a railway that offers its customers two routes (both about 1.25 miles in length). The origins of the railway date back to 1946, when John Samuel, living in a house called 'Greywood' on the Burford Estate in Walton-on-Thames in Surrey, built a 7¼ inch gauge railway in his garden, which was about 0.75 miles long. This was quite a feat in those times, as it was just after the Second World War and the country was still on rations. He named it the Greywood Central Railway and he ran it with a small team of volunteers until his death in October 1962 threw the future of the railway into doubt. The publisher Ian Allen purchased the railway, and with the help of many of the volunteers they moved to their present site in Hardwick Lane. The railway was relaunched in 1968 under the new name of the Great Cockrow Railway. The railway has expanded and grown since then and is still one of the more popular lines to be visited. On 20 October 2013 No. 1803 *River Itchen,* a Southern Railways-based 2-6-0 locomotive built in 1939, is seen alongside three other locomotives, all of which were being prepared ahead of the day's steaming. Further details can be found at www.cockcrow.co.uk.

The railway has an extensive twin route layout, but there are also over thirty steam locomotives and about half a dozen battery-electric and petrol locomotives in their fleet, many of which are privately owned but run on the railway. One of these is a 1952-built model of a Great Western Railway 2-6-0 6959 (Modified Hall) Class. Here, No. 7915 *Mere Hall* patiently awaits outside the main locomotive shed after being prepared for the day's running on 20 October 2013. The other half a dozen steam locomotives being readied for the day ahead can be seen in the background.

The coaching stock used on the railways varies from the many seen throughout the country. For instance, the carriages used on the Great Cockrow Railway are different from other railways in that people sit on the boards that go across the body of the carriage with their feet on the inside of the carriage, rather than the outside. Pictured prior to departure on a passenger working on 20 October 2013 is this example, No. 112. These coaches were the ones that came from the former railway, and because both railways had the same initials, the stock that ran on the new railway didn't need to be re-branded.

Town Park in Halton, Cheshire, WA7 6PT, is one of the few public parks in the country that boasts a well-used ski slope. Not far from the base of this slope is a railway-themed children's play area, which has been added next to the station of the Halton Miniature Railway (www.haltonminirail.weebly.com). The railway, which is a mile long, works its way around the park and comprises several passing loops, which can and do double up as sidings whenever work trains are required. On 9 August 2014 the railway's only 'steam looking' locomotive (which is actually a 2-8-0 petrol-hydraulic) poses for the camera alongside other locomotives from the fleet outside the shed building. Built in 1984, No. 3 *Buffalo Bill* has been fitted out with a steam outline to represent that of the popular American Rio Grande-style locomotive.

The Hampshire Narrow Gauge Railway Trust runs two railways at the Hampshire Buildings Preservation Trust's Burlesdon Brickworks site in Lower Swanwick, Hampshire, SO31 7HB: a 2 foot gauge line and a 7¼ inch gauge line. One of the locomotives on the latter railway was this unnumbered 2009-built 0-4-0ST, which is based on a Hunslet Quarry locomotive and was photographed with its current empty train on the site on 2 October 2011. Note the width of the 'sit-astride' carriages, which are considerably wider than those found on other railways of this gauge. Further details can be found at www.burlesdonbrickworks.org.uk.

Another railway that runs within the grounds of a popular garden centre is the High Legh Railway, which can be seen at the High Legh Garden Centre at Halliwells Brow in Cheshire, WA16 0QW. Run by Andy Higgins, it is host to about a dozen or so locomotives. One of them is this 0-4-0 petrol/battery-electric locomotive, which was built in 2013 and is heavily disguised in the steam-outlined form of *Ivor the Engine* from the popular Oliver Postgate 1958/59, and later 1975–77, children's television programme of the same name. The locomotive was pictured on 15 August 2015 and bears the letters M&L RTCL on its bodysides, the same as in the programme. The letters were the abbreviated fictional name of the company that owned *Ivor* in the series, the Merioneth & Llantisilly Rail Traction Company Limited.

The name Roger Greatrex is well known throughout the miniature railway scene as a builder of locomotives and miniature railway equipment. In 1993, at the Fletchers Garden Centre in Eccleshall, Staffordshire, ST21 6JY, he opened a 500-yard circular line he had constructed, named the Hilcote Valley Railway. One of his more easily recognisable locomotive designs is the 4-4w petrol-hydraulic locomotive, loosely based on the Union Pacific Centennial DD40X diesel-electric locomotives from the late 1960s and early 1970s. Pictured at the railway on 14 September 2013 is No. 6610 *Hercules*.

Hollybush Miniature Railway in the Hollybush Garden Centre, Shareshill, Staffordshire, WV10 7LX, runs around two small lakes and features a tunnel and an embankment on its eight-minute journey around its 950-yard length. The railway also serves a coarse fishing lake, where visiting fishermen can purchase tickets for the day and get dropped off and picked up again from the lakeside. It is operated by this uniquely liveried Roger Greatrex 4-4w petrol-hydraulic locomotive, which was seen on 14 September 2013. It was built in 1998 and, as can be seen from this picture, carries the number 645 and is branded HB Rail and Holly Bush Rail. This livery is unique in that the majority of Roger Greatrex-designed locomotives of this type carry Union Pacific livery, as seen in the previous photograph.

In the small Somerset village of Isle Abbotts can be found the 800-metre, privately owned 7¼ inch gauge Isle Abbotts Railway. The railway has been developed and extended since 2012 by the residents of the village, but it does not open to the public as other railways do on a regular basis. Having said that, they do run occasional special open days, which usually coincide with village fundraising events, and these occasions are well attended. On 28 December 2013 I attended one of these open day events and photographed the locomotives and stock that were running that day. One of these was this 1988-built Bo-Bo battery-electric locomotive, No. 5 *Churston Rambler*, which was apparently built at the Fairway Railway Workshops – although I have been so far unsuccessful in finding out any further information about where they were based.

Trenance Leisure Park in Newquay, Cornwall, TR7 2HL, is the home of the Little Western Railway, which runs on a 300-yard circular track around the inside of the park. On a lovely sunny spring day, the 1980 Mardyke-built 4-4w petrol-hydraulic locomotive (based on the popular InterCity 125 Class 43 diesel locomotive) comes around the corner with its two carriages and lone passenger, heading towards the station. The little lad thoroughly enjoyed his ride and he proclaimed in a delighted voice to the lady who was with him when he arrived at the station, 'I was the only person on the train – it was great! I had the whole train to myself, can I go around again please?' Obviously a future railway enthusiast, his declaration along with accompanying photograph occurred on 14 June 2014.

Manor Park Miniature Railway can be found in the park of the same name in Glossop, Derbyshire, SK23 oQJ. Photographed on a sunny 15 August 2015 in use at this railway is the 4w-4w battery-electric locomotive D7001 *Galahqd* (note the number is not carried). This engine was built by Cromar White Ltd in 1970, and is based on the Beyer-Peacock Maybach B-B Class 35 Hymek locomotives that were a popular sight on Britain's railways during the 1960s and early to mid-1970s.

At Barrs Lane in Knaphill, Surrey, GU21 2JW, you will find the Mizens Railway, which is operated by the Woking Miniature Railway Society. This railway is home to over twenty locomotives of steam, petrol, diesel and battery-electric types. One of the first things that you will see as you enter the site is the 'gate guardian' in the form of an ex-South African Railways 3 foot 6 inch gauge 4-8-2T steam locomotive. The railway covers about 1.5 miles of track over a large part of the 10-acre site within which it is situated. The main locomotive area has a turntable in the centre with numerous lines coming off, which lead into single-door, lockable, purpose-built sheds, as can be seen behind this 2-6-2 locomotive on 20 October 2013. The locomotive was just reaching the finishing stages of being built and will eventually be named *Oye*. More information can be found at www.mizensrailway.co.uk.

Autumn is clearly visible in this picture of a 2000-built American-style Rio Grande 2-8-0, No. 391 *Thunderhoof*, as it inches its way along the tracks on 20 October 2013 to take its place at the front of a train of passengers (just out of shot to the left of the picture). Unlike the national network, a few dozen leaves on the line don't prevent these trains from running.

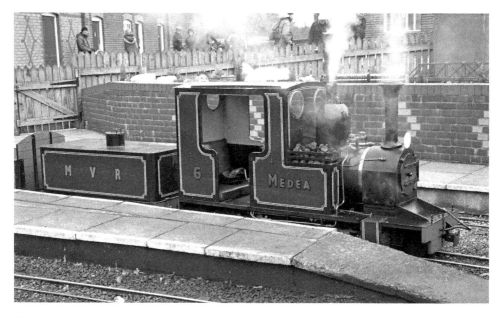

The first picture in the book was taken at the first miniature railway that I visited, and which caused me to really start to take an interest in them – the Moors Valley Railway. The locomotives used on this railway are tank engines that are designed to enable the driver to sit inside, therefore allowing running all year round. Photographed on 24 March 2013 is No. 6 *Medea,* a 2-6-2T of 1981 build, sitting at the platform awaiting its next trainload of passengers. Note the large water tank behind the locomotive and the unusual positioning of the coal bunkers (one on either side just in front of the driver's cab area).

One thing worth noting is that due to the design of the locomotives that run on the railway, they are more powerful than many of the other 7¼ inch gauge locomotives found in the country. An example of this is No. 10 *Offa*, which is a 2-6-2 built by the railway in 1991, and which has before pulled a twenty-five-carriage train carrying 198 passengers and three guards. Not many engines of this gauge can achieve a feat like that! However, on 24 March 2013, she is seen leaving the shed with a much lighter load in the form of a rake of eleven empty carriages, a barrier wagon and a guard's van, which is the standard size of a train, in readiness for the day's operations. Visit their website at www.moorsvalleyrailway.co.uk for more details on the locomotives and stock used on this railway.

In 1983, in Bught Park on the western edge of Inverness in Scotland, IV3 5SS, the most northerly public miniature railway, namely the Ness Islands Railway, opened (www.nessislandsrailway.co.uk). The railway is on Whin Island, which consists mainly of a children's play area and a boating lake. Pictured on 27 March 2016 is this 4w-4w battery-electric locomotive, No. 14 *Uncle John*, which was built in 2015. This is the second locomotive on the railway to carry this name. Note the piece of clear film over the space that is the cab window. This was necessitated by the window accidentally getting broken the day before my visit, although the circumstances regarding how were not known to me at the time.

The railway uses 'sit-astride' type carriages, and as you can see they have footwells with sides to protect the feet and ankles of the passengers. On 27 March 2016, No. C01 awaits the arrival of more passengers before the train embarks on another journey around the 950 yards of running track.

Paradise Park Garden and Leisure Centre in Newhaven, East Sussex, BN9 0DH, is where the Newhaven Miniature Railway, which runs around a 200-yard circular track, can be found. The railway, which was opened in 1989, features an unnumbered Class 35 Hymek-based 4w-4w diesel-hydraulic locomotive that was built by Mardyke Miniatures in 2011, and also a set of 'sit-in' carriages that carry the Brighton Belle livery. The packed train is seen here on 3 August 2013 as it approaches the start/finish of its route. The two eyes stuck on the cab windows of the locomotive are aimed at making the train more child-friendly, as it is a common belief that they tend to associate trains with faces as being related to *Thomas the Tank Engine* characters. I'm not really sure that actually works, because several children love riding on 'small trains', as they call them, and they more readily associate with a train if it is carrying a short but memorable name, such as *Toby, George* or *Freddy,* and so on.

The Station Road Steam Company in Lincolnshire are builders of various gauges of miniature railway locomotives. On a very wet 20 October 2013, one of their 0-4-0ST engines, named *Gentoo,* awaits departure on its 0.5-mile journey through scenic woodland on the Pinewood (Wokingham) Miniature Railway, which is located at Pinewood Leisure Centre, Wokingham, Berkshire, RG40 3AQ. It is operated by members of the Pinewood Miniature Railway Society Ltd, which was formed over twenty-five years ago. The conditions on that day are attested to by the waterproof clothing being worn by the driver of the train. Their website can be visited at www.pinewoodrailway.co.uk.

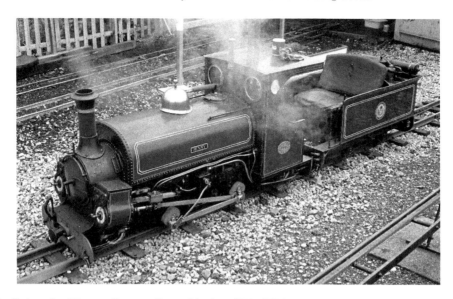

The Railway Age Heritage Centre in Crewe, Cheshire, CW1 2DB, houses a 600-yard-long miniature railway, along with standard gauge exhibits. Built in 1992 is this 2-4-0ST+T locomotive, *Jenny*, which is one of the two steam locomotives on the railway. It is seen here in between working trains on 19 July 2014. More information can be found at www.creweheritagecentre.co.uk.

The Rugby Model Engineering Society Limited run the Rainsbrook Valley Railway on a 12-acre site of land that is leased from the Borough Council. The site features a ground level 7¼ inch line and a raised elevated triple-purpose line (featuring 2½ inch, 3½ inch and 5 inch gauges). They are one of the few locations in the country that cater for 2½ inch gauge locomotives, on account of this being not an overly popular choice of gauge for many people or societies or clubs. Pictured on 13 June 2015 is *Rufus*, a 2-6w-2 petrol-mechanical locomotive that was built during the 1980s. As you can clearly see in the picture, this locomotive is a perfect example for showing that not all miniature railway locomotives are actually models of main line engines. This once again demonstrates how vast the variety is of these railways for interested enthusiasts and public alike.

The railway uses 'sit-astride' coaches that differ from many railways in that the sides of them are fully enclosed and therefore offer better protection to the legs of the general public, as can be seen in this example, No. 106, which was photographed on 13 June 2015. The single seat at the rear of the vehicle is where the train guard sits, and his flags are clearly visible. The railway is located in Onley Lane, Rugby, Warwickshire, CV22 5QD. The railway has recently been awarded the top prize of £12,000, as voted for by the public in the Tesco Bags of Help grant award scheme. The money will be used for developing the site and amenities further. For further information on the railway, including running days, go to www.rugbymes.co.uk.

South Garden Miniature Railway can be found within the complex of the National Railway Museum in York, YO26 4XJ (www.nrm.org.uk). Seen here waiting to depart on its short 150-yard journey on 7 April 2012 is this 6w-6w diesel-hydraulic locomotive, No. 55002 *The Kings Own Yorkshire Light Infantry*, which was built in 2011 by Mardyke Miniatures Ltd and is a scaled-down version of the highly popular English Electric-Napier Co-Co Class 55 Deltic diesel-electric locomotives that ran on Britain's railways for twenty years from the early 1960s until the early 1980s.

The new millennium brought lots of new challenges to many people. One of those was Geoff Jago, who built and owned a ¼ inch scale model of a Denver & Rio Grande 2-8-0 steam locomotive, which he ran regularly around the Fareham & District Society of Model Engineers club track, which was rather limited. So he decided that he would build his own miniature railway, and he spent two years scouring the Chichester and Havant areas for a suitable site, which was eventually found in the grounds of Stansted House Park in Rowlands Castle, PO9 6DX. Following on from two and a half years of building (assisted by three volunteers), the railway opened its 0.5-mile track at Easter 2005. The railway has grown substantially since then and now runs to almost a mile in an extensive layout through an arboretum and woodland, crossing over a pond and also features an impressive nine-road turntable, engine and carriage shed (complete with small workshop). Photographed on 24 September 2017, having just offloaded its passengers, is this 1982-built 4w-4w petrol-hydraulic locomotive, named *Rio Grande* (which formerly also carried the number 1982 on the cabside). For more history visit www.splr.info.

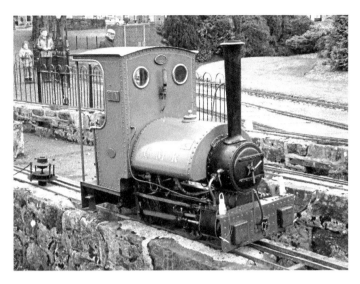

Located within the George Allan Park in Strathaven, South Lanarkshire, ML10 6EF, is the Strathaven Miniature Railway, which opened to the public for the first time in 1949. The dual-gauge (7¼ inch and 5 inch) railway is operated by members of the Strathaven Model Society Ltd. Posing for the camera (although not deliberately positioned, I might add) on 30 March 2013 is this exquisite little 0-4-0ST locomotive, which was built *c.* 1989 and is named *Eva*. Note the lines behind the locomotive that form part of the 500-yard double circular track. There is also an elevated track within this circuit.

Within Swanley Park, Swanley, Kent, BR8 7PW, a miniature railway (with a slight difference) opened to the public in 1986 – the Swanley New Barn Railway. The thing that sets this railway apart from others is that it was set up as a means of transport to provide the quickest way for moving people and their luggage from the main car park to the attractions that can also be found in the park. In order to achieve this successfully, each train also has a luggage wagon at the rear (for buggies and so on). The highly popular railway can on busy days operate three or four trains at the same time on the 900 yards of track, with one train passing the signal box on the line every thirty seconds or so. The railway is home to around twenty different locomotives (along with sheds and a workshop), and one of those locomotives is this Mardyke-built 6w-6w diesel-hydraulic model of the 1968-built Brush Co-Co diesel-electric experimental locomotive HS4000 *Kestrel*. This version was built in 1999 and is seen here devoid of any numbers or markings on 20 April 2014, due to a repaint having only been completed the day before. Worth noting is that the original locomotive was exported to Russia and was believed to have been scrapped there during the late 1980s. Many people believe that it might still exist, as trying to find confirmation of its demise is fairly difficult since it allegedly happened during the period when what is now Russia was still the Soviet Union.

The Trentham Estate in Stoke-on-Trent in Staffordshire, ST4 8AX, is well renowned for its famous gardens. It is probably a lot less known for the Trentham Fern 700-yard miniature railway. Seen on a bright sunny day on 14 September 2013 while pulling its fully loaded train of three coaches is this Roger Greatrex-built 2005 6w petrol-hydraulic locomotive, *Trentham Fern*. Worth noting is that the train comprises adults only, and apart from the two boys on the right-hand side of the wooden fence, a child is not to be seen anywhere in the picture.

Wellington Country Park Railway runs in a 500-yard circular route around the park of the same name in Riseley, Hampshire, RG7 1SP. The railway comprises of two locomotives: this one, No. 11 *Charlotte*, seen here on 3 August 2013, which is a 1990-built 0-4-0+0-4-0 diesel-hydraulic locomotive by Crowhurst Engineering and a 4w battery-electric Maxitrak Planet style engine dating from 2008. More information on the railway can be found at www.wellington-country-park.co.uk.

The Somerset resort of Weston-super-Mare has always been a popular destination for holidaymakers, boasting a pier (newly rebuilt in 2010 after a major fire destroyed the old one on 28 July 2008), a promenade with two road vehicle 'land trains' operating along it, a sea life centre and a helicopter museum, to name a few attractions. However, between 1981 and 2012 it also had the Weston Miniature Railway, which ran for over 0.75 miles around the putting green and along the promenade at the south end of the town. The railway was originally devised by miniature railways expert and author the late Robin Butterell. Sadly, the railway, like so many others, has now closed; all the track has been lifted and the stock removed. Seen during much happier days on 16 June 2010, the railway's steam-outlined 4w petrol-hydraulic locomotive, No. 1 *Dylan*, which was built in 1985 as a collaboration between Roger Greatrex and the operator of the railway, Ron Bullock, ferries its trainload of happy smiling children (and one lone woman) across Beach Lawns, heading back to the start of the line, while a group of adults partake in some refreshments behind them. The railway also had a larger engine in the shape of a 4w-4w petrol-hydraulic. This locomotive, No. 3 *Dennis*, was last seen by myself stabled in March 2016 outside of the engine shed of the Ness Islands Railway in Inverness – which is about as far away from its old stamping ground as you could possibly get.

Bruce Whalley operates a couple of miniature railways in the country, and one of those is the Weston Park Railway, near Shifnal in Staffordshire, TF11 8LE. Besides being an operator, Bruce has also successfully built a number of locomotives as well. Seen here at the aforementioned railway is this example 4w-4w diesel-hydraulic, *Merlin*, which was built by him in 2000. It is the main working engine at the railway (although many visiting locomotives can also be found during the summer months), running here on the 1.2 miles of line, where it was photographed on 9 August 2014, waiting to start work for the day.

White Post Corner, Farnsfield, Nottinghamshire, NG22 8HX, is where you will find the childrens' Wheelgate Adventure Park and its miniature railway (www.wheelgatepark.com). On 26 August 2013, No. 2 *Mickey* prepares to depart with a train full of passengers on its 400-yard journey around a part of the park complex. This locomotive was built by Roger Greatrex, and is vastly different to his Union Pacific design locomotives, seen earlier in this book. This 4w-2w petrol-hydraulic locomotive was built in 1999 and is unique by the fact that it has not only been given a steam-outlined body shell, but it also features the synchronised sound of an actual steam locomotive, which can be clearly heard as the train moves along.

The Woodseaves Miniature Railway can be found at a garden plants nursery near Market Drayton in Shropshire, TF9 2AS. The railway is home to two locomotives (one steam and one petrol-hydraulic), and the track is just under 0.5 miles long. The owners do welcome groups and clubs, but advise that you must telephone in advance before visiting (details are on their website, www.woodseavesminirail.co.uk). 9 August 2014 found the railway's steam locomotive *Jean*, which is a 1994 built 0-4-0, sat languishing outside of the engine shed and combined workshop. The day before my visit it had been used for a private party on the railway. Note the open smokebox door and the ash on the solebar from where it had been cleaned out earlier during the day.

Chapter 5 – 8¼ Inch Gauge

This is an extremely rare and seldom-found gauge. I only know so far of one working locomotive in this gauge and it is featured here.

Near the beginning of the previous chapter there is a photograph of one of the 7¼ inch gauge locomotives at the Bankside Miniature Railway in Hampshire. The railway also has this rare 8¼ inch gauge locomotive, a 1924-built 2-6-2T engine, No. 815 *Carolyn*, which is seen here inside the railway's loco shed on 12 October 2013. This loco runs on a 300-yard elevated balloon loop track.

Chapter 6 – 8½ Inch Gauge

This is another of those rare and seldom-found gauges, and once again I only know of one working locomotive in this gauge, which is featured here.

Very little is known about the history of this unusual gauge 0-6-0T locomotive, except that it was built *c.* 1936 by Claude Jessett. It now resides at the Claude Jessett Trust Company headquarters at Tinkers Park in Hadlow Down, East Sussex, TN22 4HS (www.tinkerspark.com), where it runs on a short length of track alongside the 2 foot gauge Great Bush Railway. On 4 August 2012 it was pictured in between carrying passengers, although why the smokebox door is open is not quite clear as it was not the end of the running day.

Chapter 7 – 9 Inch Gauge

Another unusual gauge that is rarely seen – so much so that there is only one location in the UK that is open to the public regularly and uses this gauge.

Brogdale Farm in Faversham, Kent, ME13 8XZ, is the home of the Faversham Miniature Railway Society's 9 inch gauge railway (www.favershamminiaturerailway.co.uk). It is the only railway that is open regularly to the public that uses this gauge, and its 900-yard complex winds its way through the apple orchards on the farm. Pictured on 19 April 2014 (as are all the photographs in this chapter) was this newly completed 6w-6w petrol-hydraulic locomotive, which is based on the Brush Type 2 Class 31 A1A-A1A diesel-electric. Here, No. 31466, sporting the English, Welsh & Scottish Railways red livery with yellow stripe, waits for more passengers to get on board before setting off on another trip around the orchards.

This 4w petrol-hydraulic shunting locomotive (with a Honda engine in it) was built in 1990 by Iron Horse Engineering and loosely resembles the industrial diesel-mechanical locomotives built by the Hunslet Engine Company in Leeds. No. 5 is seen shyly peering out of the engine shed.

The railway hosts a variety of coaches, and this example, No. 5, is a 'ride-in' open type designed to carry six people and a train guard. Note the red flag in the rear section. Also note how the guard has a cushion and yet the passengers have to sit on the uncomfortable-looking bare slatted pieces of wood.

Another 'ride-in' coach on the railway is No. 12 *Bob*, which can seat twelve people. Note how the seats at either end of the vehicle are stepped, meaning that the passengers there sit higher up than those in the middle section.

Coach No. 50 is one of three coaches on the railway that afford the passengers a little more comfort, as it is a 'ride-in' closed version. These coaches are usually, however, only used when the weather is inclement. Note the look-outs on the doors on the right-hand end of the vehicle; these are used in the same way that those on standard gauge coaches were, in that they enable the guard to look down the entire length of the train safely, eliminating the need to get out of the coach.

The railway also has what very few miniature railways do – a set of articulated coaches. These vehicles had been lying neglected in a field for many years and the volunteers on the railway, apart from removing the rust and other signs of decay, built new bogies for the vehicles, replaced side panels and fitted them with padded seats. This example was pictured, shortly after being repainted, behind the newly built Class 31 locomotive, which is seen waiting for passengers for what was to be the first public run for both engine and stock. These carriages are unique in that they also contain access to, bizarrely, an online casino.

Chapter 8 – 9½ Inch Gauge

One of the earliest gauges when miniature railways started to take off in this country. However, in time it became unpopular with operators and they preferred to either go with the 7¼ inch or the 10¼ inch gauges instead, making locomotives of this gauge quite rare to find these days.

The Hall Leys Miniature Railway is operated by the Miniature Railway Co. Ltd and it runs a 200-yard straight track in a corner of Hall Leys Park. It is one of the very few miniature railways open to the public that uses this gauge. Power is provided in the form of this 6w diesel-hydraulic locomotive. Named *Little David*, it was built by renowned locomotive builders Coleby Simkins in 1974. Prior to this locomotive the railway was operated by a steam locomotive that was built in 1948, which can be seen in the museum building at Swanwick Junction on the Midland Railway Centre. The railway can be found in the park of the same name in Matlock, Derbyshire, DE4 3AT. This photograph and the one that follows were both taken on 15 August 2015.

The coaches used on this relatively short railway comprise three permanently coupled vehicles, with two 'sit-astride' ones at each end of this rather unique 'ride-in' open variety. This vehicle is unusual in that it has eight single seats that can seat sixteen people, but the seats all face the direction of travel, whereas the standard practice on coaches of this type on miniature lines is to have the passengers sat in separate compartments facing each other.

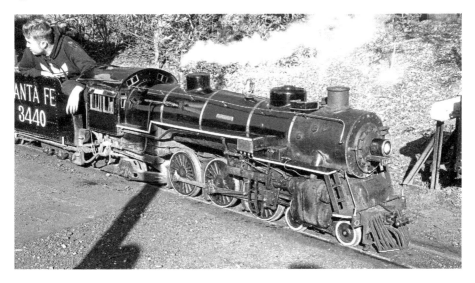

Another public railway that operates using 9½ inch gauge track can be found in the South Marine Park in South Shields, Tyne and Wear, NE33 2PE, called the Lakeshore Railroad. Its 550-yard circular track runs around a lake and has three locomotives that are all notable scaled-down versions of the originals. No. 3440 *Mountaineer* is seen here prior to departure on another circuit of the lake. This 4-6-2 1968-built engine is a 1/6 scale of an Atcheson, Topeka & Santa Fe Railroad prototype locomotive. Baking in the autumn sunshine on 19 October 2014, it waits to begin its journey around the lake.

The coaches used on the railway are all 'ride-in' open ones that can seat eight people. They are an all-metal design that come complete with chains instead of doors and are in different colours. All nine of the coaches do not carry a number, but do have some rather unusual names, this example being *The Blind Miller*. The others of the same design are named *The Fen Tiger, The Iron Facade, The Mallen Streak, The Menagerie, The Moth* and *The Nice Bloke*.

The coaches that convey the guards are also different from other railways, in that the guard is stood on a platform at the rear of the vehicle, which means that no passenger seats are lost to accommodate him. The railway has two of these vehicles; this one, named *The Whip*, and one other, named *The Invitation*. Note the platform at the rear for the train guard and the 'mouseholes' in the sides, which give access to the axles. For some unknown reason, these holes are only found on the two vehicles of this type.

Chapter 9 – 10¼ Inch Gauge

This gauge is the second most popular in the UK, and like the 7¼ inch gauge there are a few locations that have extensive layouts in this gauge, including the Rudyard Lake Railway in Leek, the Bickington Steam Railway near Newton Abbot, Stapleford Park near Melton Mowbray and the Lakeside Country Park in Eastleigh, which is dual gauged with 7¼ inch.

The first picture in Chapter Four was of a locomotive that belonged to a member of the Saffron Walden & District Society of Model Engineers, who operate alongside the Audley End Miniature Railway, which is a 10¼ inch gauge railway of 1 mile in length. Pictured on 21 April 2014, having stopped to take on water from the nearby water tower, was this 1977 David Curwen-built Denver & Rio Grande 2-8-2 locomotive, No. 489 *Sara Lucy*, which is seen waiting to couple onto a waiting train of people, who are all eager to get their ride underway. More details can be found at www.audley-end-railway.co.uk.

In Stover, near Newton Abbot in Devon, a person can find themselves in the highly popular Trago Mills Shopping and Leisure Centre, TQ12 6JB, which is home to the very extensive 2.25-mile Bickington Steam Railway. After leaving the station, the line descends across an impressive twenty-three-pier (arch) viaduct and then loops across itself several times before climbing back up again. The railway is such an intricate and brilliantly designed one, and at one point on the journey around the centre there are six parallel tracks – all of which are on different levels. Dealing with one of the lesser complex parts on the railway (namely the turntable) is the 1984 Coleby-Simkins-built 2-6-0 steam locomotive *Alice*, seen as she turns around to go back to the head of the train to start another run of the circuit on 21 July 2012.

The railway uses covered 'ride-in' coaches with three compartments in each one, which can seat twelve people, as seen in this unnumbered example on 21 July 2012. Note the clerestory style roofs, which are not a common feature on miniature railway coaching stock.

The Bressingham Steam Preservation Co. Ltd (www.bressingham.co.uk) are responsible for the operating of the Steam Museum & Gardens in Diss, Norfolk, IP22 2AB. Apart from the standard gauge exhibits, fairground rides and several vehicles that were used in the BBC comedy programme series *Dad's Army*, there are three different narrow gauge and miniature railways (2 foot, 15 inch and 10¼ inch). On a rain-sodden 3 April 2010, this 1995-built 0-4-0ST locomotive, No. 1 *Alan Bloom,* is seen ready to do another run on its 700 yard-long line. The torrential rain is coming down and is so intense (why I am stood in open ground taking a picture in these conditions?) that it gives the impression that the photograph itself is so old and has been so badly stored that it is covered in several long vertical scratches.

Photographed on 12 August 2017 is this Fenlow-built 1972 4w-4w diesel-hydraulic locomotive, named *Conway Castle,* which looks like a crossover between a Brush Type 4 Class 47 and a Brush Type 5 Class 56 Co-Co engine. It was seen in between giving rides to the public at the Cassiobury Park Railway in Watford, Hertfordshire, WD18 7LG. Unlike most railways found running around public parks, this railway has a fleet comprising three working locomotives.

Delamont Country Park in Kilyleagh, County Down, Northern Ireland (www.delamontcountrypark.com) has a 1,000-yard circular route miniature railway that runs within it. Like so many other railways of this type, the motive power is provided by the means of one sole locomotive, and in this case it is this 1984-built 4w petrol-hydraulic, *Freddy*, which is seen here waiting to start on another circuit on 4 April 2015. *Freddy* has been given a steam-outlined body and what seems to be have become obligatory where rides aimed at children are concerned, a *Thomas the Tank Engine*-style face on the front. Note how the track is not bedded down in ballast, but seems to be somehow attached to a concrete pathway instead. I'm not certain if the sleepers are attached somehow by bolts to the concrete or if they are embedded into it. This unusual setup is normally only found where portable railways operate and is very rarely seen at permanent locations.

Quite extensive earthworks were required at the Brooklands Pleasure Park in East Worthing, West Sussex, BN15 8RR, in order to get the track on a level course prior to the opening here in 1965 of the miniature railway, which was operated by a steam locomotive for a short while. The motive power these days is very different on the now named Diddly's Miniature Railway and is provided by two steam-outlined and heavily made up 4w-4w diesel-hydraulic locomotives. Even the coaches are heavily disguised, as can be seen in this picture of *Diddly-Dum,* which was built in 1985 and was in service when seen on a sunny 3 August 2013. The other locomotive, named *Diddly-Dee,* which was not built until twenty-four years later, in 2009, was inside the maintenance and loco shed. It is identical in looks to this one, but is in different colours. The locomotives apparently represent the characters from a children's book. More information on this and the railway can be found at www.thediddlys.co.uk.

Eastleigh Lakeside Steam Railway can be found in the Lakeside Country Park, Eastleigh, Hampshire, SO50 5PE (www.steamtrain.co.uk). It comprises a circular dual-gauge (7¼ inch and 10¼ inch) 1.75-mile-long layout and is home to over twenty locomotives. One of those locomotives is this 1983-built 2-4-2, No. 7, which was modelled on a Sandy River Railroad locomotive from the 1800s amd named, appropriately, *Sandy River.* It was seen preparing for a day's running on the railway on 24 March 2013.

The Exmouth Fun Park, EX8 2AY, can be found along the seafront of this coastal town in Devon. Among its attractions there is a 150-yard circular miniature railway that runs around some of the amusements in the park. The railway first opened to the public in 1949 and during the 1950s and '60s it was operated by steam locomotives. The traction these days is provided by this 4w diesel-mechanical locomotive, *Exmouth Express*, which was built in 1978 and was seen between operations on 8 September 2013. During the late 1960s and early 1970s a company called Shepperton Metal Products was building miniature railway locomotives; one type in their 10 ¼ inch gauge range for which they were renowned was called the Meteor; they were named *Meteor I*, *Meteor II* etc. During 1977 two locomotives (namely *Meteor III* and *Meteor VII*) were operating in Buckfastleigh, Devon, when it was noticed that *Meteor III* was beginning to rust very badly and so a decision was taken to scrap it. However, it wasn't scrapped but was purchased by Geoffrey Kichenside, who rebuilt it into this example, using one of the cabs and part of the frames and also, it is believed, the gearbox.

The locomotive *Meteor VII* was mentioned in the previous image as being at Buckfastleigh and sometime during its time there it was involved in an accident that severely damaged one cab and the loco was deemed to be scrap. Once again, though, the loco wasn't scrapped but was purchased by the operator of the Knebworth Park Miniature Railway, which until 2012 ran for 700 yards around the grounds of Knebworth House in Hertfordshire. This operator also purchased the remaining cab from *Meteor III*, and that became the front cab of this locomotive named *Midget* while the frames and the undamaged cab from *Meteor VII* were used for the remainder of this 2001-built 4w petrol-mechanical example, which was seen on 12 August 2017 at its new home, the Hatfield Farm Miniature Railway in Hertfordshire. This loco and the other two that make up the operating fleet on this railway all worked on the Knebworth Park Railway. Further information on this new location can be found at www.hatfieldparkfarm.co.uk.

Nene Park in Peterborough, Cambridgeshire, PE2 5UU, is where you can enjoy a ride on the Ferry Meadows Miniature Railway. This 700-yard line, which was opened in 1979, is home to two steam-outlined locomotives (one petrol and one diesel), and this magnificent-looking steam locomotive. This 0-4-0ST, modelled on a Darjeeling Himalayan Railway engine, was completed in 2012 and was seen on the railway's turntable during its first public running on 16 February 2013, carrying the number 44. For further information on the railway visit www.ferrymeadowsrailway.co.uk.

At the Mill of Logierait Farm in Pitlochry, Perthshire, PH9 0LH, the unique Highland Light Railway can be found. The railway is unusual in that it is not a traditional tourist style attraction – it is actually a working railway used for farm work and it carries visitors to the local farmers' markets that are normally held three or four times a year (www.railwayfarm.com). The owners of the railway, Peter and Fiona Guinan, sadly lost their youngest son, Andrew, aged twenty-three, following an accident in an off-road event he was taking part in during 2011. Although this was a great loss to the family, they are funding and supporting a worthwhile charity in the form of the Tayside Mountain Rescue Association in memory of their son. Members of the Cardiff & Avonside Railway Society enjoyed a privately arranged visit to this unique railway on Good Friday, 25 March 2016. Here they observed this 2001-built 4w-4w diesel-hydraulic steam-outlined locomotive *Spirit of Orm*, which was formerly named *Claude the Colonel*.

The railway uses 'ride-in' open coaches to ferry the visitors to the farmers' markets, such as this example seen on 25 March 2016. At that time the railway was in the process of converting a couple of these coaches to covered vehicles. Evidence of this can be seen in the background, where an open coach can be clearly observed with the framework attached that will hold the roof and sides of the completed vehicle following its conversion.

The Lappa Valley Steam Railway, based in St Newlyn East in Cornwall, TR8 5HZ (www.lappavalley. co.uk), has an assortment of activities where children of all ages can enjoy themselves. These include a Crazy Golf course, a canoeing lake and nature trails, to name a few. There are also three miniature railways, all of which are of different gauges: the Steam Railway itself, which is 15 inch gauge and is 1.25 miles in length; the 0.5-mile-long 10¼ inch Newlyn Branchline; and the 350-yard 7¼ inch gauge circular railway. Photographed at the head of a packed train on the Newlyn Branchline on 19 June 2011 was this 0-6-0 diesel-hydraulic locomotive named *Eric*, which was built by the locomotive manufacturing company Alan Keef Ltd in 2008.

The 500-yard-long circular Melton Mowbray Miniature Railway runs around the bowling green and children's play area in the Leicester Road Sportsground in Melton Mowbray, Leicestershire, LE13 0DA. On a bright and sunny 26 August 2013, the railway's one and only resident, a 1968-built 2w-2w petrol-mechanical locomotive, No. 1, is seen here with its driver taking payment from a young family in readiness to take them on their trip around its circuit in the 'ride-in' open coaches, while other youngsters look on in wonder.

The sign in the background reads 'Feed the Ducks and Fish Here', and it is one of the many things that children are encouraged to partake in and enjoy at the Pettitts Animal Adventure Park in Reedham, Norfolk, NR13 3UA (www.pettittsadventurepark.co.uk). The park also has a 0.5-mile miniature railway as one of its attractions. The railway was originally built in 1989 as a 7¼ inch gauge line, but this was changed eleven years later in 2000 to the 10¼ inch gauge that it is today. Seen waiting for its next trainload of families to get on board on 12 August 2007 is the park's own 1990-built steam-outlined unnumbered 4w-4w diesel-hydraulic locomotive, which carries the simple name *Pettitts* on the imitation smokebox door.

Looking resplendent in the summer sunshine on 7 July 2013 at the Lodmoor Country Park's Rio Grande Railway in Weymouth, Dorset, DT4 7SX, is this 1990 Severn Lamb-built Rio Grande Class 2-6-0 diesel-hydraulic steam-outlined locomotive, No. 1890.

Royal Victoria Country Park in Netley, Hampshire, SO31 5GA, was once the largest military hospital in the world, with buildings that stretched for over 0.25 miles in length. The hospital was served by its own standard gauge railway station, of which the chapel building remains as a museum. Today the park is home to the Royal Victoria Railway (www.royalvictoriarailway.co.uk), which replaced a previous, much shorter railway of the same gauge. This new railway opened in 1996, using a single locomotive and some hired coaches. Since that time they have built an extension of half a mile (making the circular railway just over a mile long), a new engine shed and a turntable. The coaches are all built on-site in the specially constructed workshops, and the railway is home to a dozen locomotives, which were purchased from other railways, some in a derelict condition. Seen on 24 March 2013 with a rake of three 'ride-in' covered coaches is one of them in the form of this scale model of a British Railways C-C Type 4 Class 52 Western diesel-hydraulic locomotive. This 6w-6w diesel-hydraulic version, D1000 *Western Independence,* was built in 1964 by renowned builder of miniature railway locomotives the late David Curwen (who sadly passed away aged ninety-eight in May 2011) for use on the now closed Margate Pier Railway.

Running for 1.5 miles along the track bed of a section of the standard gauge North Staffordshire Railway is the Rudyard Lake Steam Railway, Leek, Staffordshire, ST13 8PF (www.rlsr.org). This railway, which opened in 1985, is home to about ten locomotives, including three from the now closed Isle of Mull Railway. Half of the locomotive fleet carry names from Arthurian legend; however, the two examples shown here, photographed on 15 September 2012, do not. Nearest the camera is the 1993-built 2-6-2T engine, named *Victoria*, and behind it is a 1952 David Curwen-built 4-4-2, No. 196 *Waverley*. Note that although these locomotives have both been built to run on the same 10¼ inch gauge track, the differences in the scales used by their makers is clearly evident in this picture, with the David Curwen model being dwarfed by the much larger 1993-built locomotive.

In 2000 at the Pulborough Garden Centre in West Sussex, RH20 1DS, the South Downs Light Railway opened its 10¼ inch gauge line. Previously there was a 7¼ inch gauge miniature railway on this site, named Riverview, which closed in the mid-1990s. The new railway was extended in 2006 and its current 1,100-yard circular route features a deep cutting, which it passes through as part of the ride. Seen outside of the engine shed, waiting to start the day's running on 4 August 2012, was the aptly named *Pulborough*. This 0-4-2T engine was built in 2004 by the Exmoor Steam Railway from Bratton Fleming in North Devon and is one of three locomotives built by them that can be seen on the railway.

Seen on 4 August 2012, waiting to start the day's running, are two of the four-compartment 'ride-in' open-sided bogie coaches that the railway uses. There are three of these vehicles and two that are fully enclosed, as well as seven four-compartment 'ride-in' open coaches and a goods wagon that has been converted for passenger use.

Under the guidance of the 2nd Lord Gretton, the stately house and grounds of Stapleford Park, near Melton Mowbray, LE14 2SF, opened its miniature railway in 1958 as an additional attraction to the estate, which had opened to the public five years earlier. Using two David Curwen-built 4-4-2 steam locomotives, which had formerly worked on the miniature railway in Bognor Regis, the railway was extended numerous times. After the 1961 season the number of passengers being carried was over 21,000 and a third locomotive was required to keep up with demand. That locomotive was this 1962-built Curwen & Newbery Warship locomotive D100 *The White Heron*, which is seen here at one of the railway's public open days on 26 August 2013. Following the death of the 2nd Lord Gretton in 1982, the railway was closed to the public and put into safe storage. The house was sold in 1985 and is now a country house hotel and sports leisure complex (although the railway and estate remained with the family). Following the death of the 3rd Lord Gretton in 1989, the railway looked to be finished. However, in 1992 Lady Gretton agreed to allow a small group of enthusiasts to take over the running of the railway, much of which had to be rebuilt, and so the Friends of the Stapleford Miniature Railway was formed with Lady Gretton as their chairperson, and they currently hold two public open days a year (www.fsmr.org.uk). The railway now runs for 1.25 miles – a far cry from its inaugural opening on 18 May 1958, when the length was 2,000 feet. Also worth noting is the stately home also had a drive-through lion reserve within its grounds and two scale 45-foot-long passenger-carrying liners that operated on the estate's lake.

Described as being 'one of the most ambitious and elaborate miniature railways built' was the ill-fated Surrey Border & Camberley Railway. In was built in 1938 as the brainchild of wealthy London merchant banker and enthusiast Alexander Kinloch, and cost a staggering (at the time) £16,000. It was a 1.5-mile double-tracked line that offered people a twelve-minute ride through open fields from Farnborough Green to Camberley. It was operated by a fleet of twelve steam locomotives, many of which were built by H. C. S. Bullock, who was a local engineer, designer and locomotive builder. The railway was placed in receivership in 1939 and most of the engines were sold, although the remainder of the railway (including the track, buildings and coaches) remained in situ throughout the war, becoming abandoned and neglected – and it is surprising to find that the government didn't remove the track and use the metal to aid in the war effort. The whole thing was later dismantled and removed after the war had ended. Although the railway no longer exists, the majority of its locomotives do, and can be found at various miniature railways throughout the country. This example, No. 2005 *Silver Jubilee*, was seen in the workshops of the Eastleigh Lakeside Steam Railway on 24 March 2013.

Locomotive No. 2 *Basil the Brigadier* was built by Kitson & Co. in 1938 exclusively for the Surrey Border & Camberley Railway. Like many others following the railway's closure in 1939, when Kinloch was called up for military service, and after losing £2,000 in the first operating year, this example survived and was sold on. It is pictured here on the back of a road trailer at the Statfold Barn Railway in Tamworth on 22 September 2007, where it was awaiting transportation to its current home at the Royal Victoria Railway in Netley, Hampshire.

Pictured inside the workshops of the Friends of the Stapleford Miniature Railway on 26 August 2013 was this unidentified coach from the Surrey Border & Camberley Railway. These vehicles were unique in themselves, in that to enable the passengers to board and alight the train, the doors were made one sheet of lightweight aluminium folded across the coach body and hinged on one side, which had to be lifted upwards.

The East Midland Zoological Society not only operate the Twycross Zoo – The World Primate Centre, near Atherstone in Leicestershire, CV9 3PX (www.twycrosszoo.org), they also operate the 650-yard circular miniature railway that runs around within the grounds. The railway is powered by this 1983 Rio Grande 2-8-0 diesel-hydraulic steam-outlined locomotive built by Severn Lamb (UK) Ltd, works number 22.2.83, which is seen in between giving rides on 26 August 2013.

Photographed on 26 August 2013, this coach is of the fairly standard type used for these railways, in that they are normally a four-compartment ride-in open-sided bogie, which is built by the same builder as the locomotive (Severn Lamb in this instance) and are supplied at the same time. The colour of the roof canopy is of the customer's own preference, but are usually bright colours; in this case, yellow.

Vanstone Woodland Railway was opened in 1986 and operates within the grounds of Vanstone Park Garden Centre, Codicote, Hertfordshire, SG4 8TH. The railway, which is operated by Stuart Madgin, is 550 yards long and loops its way around woodland, which includes some steep gradients at the rear of the garden centre. At the time of my visit, on 12 August 2017, the 1970-built Shepperton Metal Products 2-4w-2 petrol-mechanical locomotive *Meteor V* was standing in the bright afternoon sunshine. This locomotive formerly ran on the Knebworth Park Miniature Railway and is one of four 'Meteor' types found on the railway. Visit www.vanstonerailway.co.uk for more details, including operating times.

In Pitsea, Essex, the extensive Wat Tyler Country Park, SS16 4UH, can be found, which includes a marina, a boat museum, an RSPB wildlife garden and visitor centre and a 10¼ inch gauge 1-mile-long miniature railway, which works its way around the perimeter of the park, serving all of the above, as its attractions. Seen here on 21 April 2014, and sporting its new 'all-over green livery, with yellow ends', is the railway's Brush Type 2 Class 31 4w-4 petrol-mechanical locomotive, which is awaiting to have its number, 31327, reapplied following its re-paint.

The Wells & Walsingham Light Railway at Wells-next-the-Sea in Norfolk, NR23 1QB, has the distinction of being the first railway of this gauge to obtain a Light Railway Order, as well as that it is the longest of this gauge in the world, being 4 miles long from end to end. The railway was opened in 1982 and runs along a former standard gauge track bed from Wells-next-the-Sea to Walsingham on the Norfolk coast. Pictured preparing to depart on a journey on 11 August 2007 is one of the railway's 2-6-0+0-6-2 Garrett-style locomotives. This example, No. 3 *Norfolk Hero*, was built in 1986, and looks rather resplendent in its white-lined blue livery. The second locomotive was built in 2011, No. 6 *Norfolk Heroine*. More information regarding the railways can be found at www.wwlr.co.uk.

Wells-next-the-Sea does in fact have two miniature railways, both of which are of 10¼ inch gauge. There is the one mentioned previously, and the much smaller (just over a mile long) Wells Harbour Railway, NR23 1DR. This railway is the older of the two lines, as it was opened in 1976 and it runs from the harbour, alongside Beach Road and to Pinewoods, and provides a very useful transport service to holidaymakers staying in a caravan site at the northern end of the town. 11 August 2007 found the 2005 Alan Keef Ltd-built 0-6-0 steam-outlined diesel-hydraulic locomotive *Howard* as it transports a fully laden four-coach train of holidaymakers south towards the town's harbour station on a sunny afternoon.

In one part of the County of Wiltshire, near Westbury, can be found 80 acres of historic broad-leaved woodland, namely the Brokerswood Country Park, BA13 4EH. On part of this massive site you can find the 600-yard-long Woodland Railway. The railway runs from the main car park of the site to the children's adventure playground at Adventure Land station. The railway's only locomotive, a 1987 Mardyke Miniatures-built 4w-4w diesel-hydraulic, *Amelia*, was seen here on 26 September 2010, waiting to take more children to their playground. Apart from the locomotive, coaches and rails, all structures on the railway are constructed entirely from wood; this includes stations, an embankment and a bridge, the evidence of which can clearly be seen in the picture.

Chapter 10 – 12 Inch Gauge

The most popular railway that operates using this gauge is the Ruslip Lido Railway in Hillingdon, Greater London. They are in fact one of the very few (if not the only one) to operate this gauge of railway on a regular basis to the public.

After the Second World War, the Grand Union Canal Company, who were the owners of 1811-built Ruislip Lido in Hillingdon, Greater London, HA4 7TY, wanted to turn the Lido into a general tourist attraction (following on from the former reservoir becoming a health spa in 1936), so in 1945 they added an artificial beach and a miniature railway. The length of the line was 1,000 yards and the Grand Union Canal Company decided that the gauge of the railway was going to be of a rather unusual 12 inches, and that the first locomotive was to be a 4-4-2 steam locomotive named *Prince Edward*, which was built in 1935. By 1960 the steam engine was getting rather worn out and it was replaced by a petrol-electric modelled on an American locomotive. Thirteen years later it was replaced by this 4w-4 diesel-hydraulic locomotive, *Robert*, which was built by Severn Lamb based on a David Curwen design. It represents a BR Class 52 Western diesel-hydraulic locomotive, and was seen hiding in the loco shed on 12 August 2017.

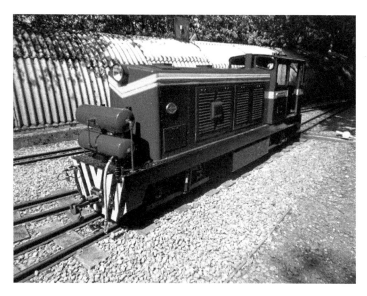

Following an accident in 1978, in which several passengers were injured, the end looked to be in sight for the railway, despite its popularity. However, Hillingdon Council, who were now responsible for the Lido, found the money to put the necessary safety measures in place, which enabled the railway to keep running. These days councils would close the attraction down forever in a knee-jerk reaction, deeming it unsafe to be operated, but thankfully forty years ago people had more common sense. So safety measures were put in place and the council also sought volunteers to not only help with the running of the railway, but to take it over completely. As a result, in 1980 the Ruislip Lido Railway Society Ltd was formed and they took over the running of the railway, which they still do today. The society decided that more locomotives were required and the first of these was this 4w-4w diesel-hydraulic, No. 5 *Lady of the Lakes*, which is pictured in the sunshine outside of the engine shed. This locomotive was built in 1986 by the Ravenglass & Eskdale Railway in Cumbria.

The railway is the longest 12 inch gauge line in the UK, and as far as I am aware the only one operating on a regular basis that is open to the public. In 1998 the society built this 2-4-oST+T oil-fired locomotive in the workshops onsite. This locomotive, No. 6 *Mad Bess*, has the capacity should it be required to be re-gauged to 15 inch.

The last locomotive that was purchased by the railway was this diesel-mechanical version. No. 9 *John Rennie* was built in 2004, and was seen on 12 August 2017, being turned around on the turntable at Rusilip Lido station, having just come in on the first train of the day. Worth noting is that the original steam locomotive that worked the railway back in the beginning was still extant in 2010, although its whereabouts then and now eight years later is currently unknown to the author.

The railway is as popular today as it was during its early years, carrying in excess of 65,000 passengers a year, and the coaching stock reflects these numbers. Pictured at Ruislip Lido station was No. 251, which has had one of the side panels removed in order to accommodate a party of disabled children (many in wheelchairs) after they had chartered the train as they do every year. The railway has ten of these four-compartment ride-in enclosed vehicles, all of which are used in the height of the busy period during the school holidays. Aside from these coaches, the railway also has six ride-in open compartment versions.

Due to the high numbers of passengers that use the railway, there was often no room in which to transport wheelchairs, pushchairs and shopping trolleys, so the railway converted two of their open passenger coaches to buggy wagons, allowing people to travel in comfort without obstacles in their way. During very busy periods these wagons will be stacked high with pushchairs and so on. On the first train of the day wagon No. 307 was empty, but by mid-morning it was full to overflowing.

The railway has about a dozen assorted freight vehicles, which are used for ongoing maintenance and upkeep of the line, ranging from tipping skip wagons and flat beds to a purpose-built generator wagon and this example, No. 506, which is a staff and tool wagon. The staff working on the track sit in the compartments at the front nearest the camera and the tools (picks, shovels, brooms, etc.) are all stored in the rear compartment with a lockable fold-down flap. Note the ear-defenders and the first aid station that is also located at the rear of the staff compartments. For more information and history on this fantastic railway visit www.ruisliplidorailway.org.

Chapter 11 – 12¼ Inch Gauge

This gauge is usually considered the penultimate one of the rideables, and is operated by a few locations in the country. It gives the operator scope to use large-looking locomotives that can run on a fairly lightweight track.

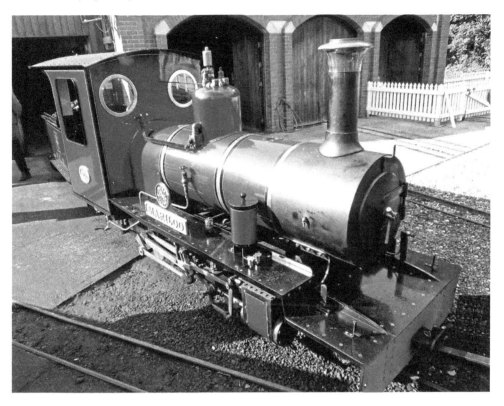

Similar to the 9½ inch gauge, there are only a small handful of public railways that operate using 12¼ inch gauge. The Exbury Gardens Railway in the Hampshire New Forest, SO45 1AZ (www.exbury.co.uk), which winds its way through the 200-acre spectacular and word-famous Rothchild Gardens on its 1.25 miles of track is one of those. The motive power used on the railway comes in the form of three Exmoor Steam Railway-built steam locomotives, with one diesel engine being used as a shunter/back up if required. Pictured on 12 October 2013 outside of the engine shed in the autumn sunshine is this 2-6-2, named *Mariloo*, which is the newest loco on the line, being built in 2008.

The railway opened to the public in 2001 and the first steam locomotive that they acquired was this 0-6-2T named *Rosemary*, which was specially built for them by Exmoor Steam Railway in North Devon. She is seen here waiting to depart on 12 October 2013 with another trainload of passengers.

The oldest locomotive owned by the railway is this 1994 4w diesel-hydraulic engine, which is the only item of rolling stock on the railway that doesn't carry a female name. *Eddy* was posing for the camera in the autumn sunshine, having been taken out of the shed on 12 October 2013 by the operator to purposefully enable a better photograph.

The railway uses a fleet of ten ride-in four-compartment open-sided roofed bogie coaches, all of which follow the lead of the steam locomotives and are adorned with ladies' names, hand-painted on the side of each one. Here is example *Jocelynne*, which, like all the carriages, also has a guard's compartment at the rear as it waits for its next load of passengers. The hand-painted name can be seen on the second panel.

Mewsbrook Park in Littlehampton, West Sussex, BN16 2LX, is home to the 800-yard 4w-4w diesel-hydraulic-powered Littlehampton Miniature Railway (www.littlehamptonrailway.co.uk). This railway has the particular boast of being the oldest of this gauge in the country and has been running since 1948. The railway, like others, has had its fair share of highs and lows, and like others from the same period has seen several different locomotives being used throughout the years, starting with steam and moving on to diesel. The latest guardian in charge of hauling the trains is this 2007-built engine D1 *Green Dragon*, which was photographed inside on the shed after the day's running on 3 August 2013.

In the historic town of Buxton in Derbyshire is the Pavilion Gardens Park, SK17 6BE, where the miniature railway bearing the same name can be found. There has been a railway here since 1972, although it was formerly a 10¼ inch gauge line; it was rebuilt during the 1999/2000 winter to the 12¼ inch gauge that it is today. Running for 300 yards in a circular layout powered by a purpose-built Alan Keef Ltd 0-6-0 diesel-hydraulic locomotive and coaches, it passes over two bridges that cross a stream. Seen here crossing one of those bridges on 15 August 2015 is *Edward Milner*. Worth noting is that the steam-outlined body of a previous gauge locomotive operated here can be seen at the Vanstone Woodland Railway that was covered in Chapter Eight of this book.

Chapter 12 – 15 Inch Gauge

The interesting thing about this gauge is that it is not only the highest gauge that can be classified as a rideable miniature, but it is the lowest gauge that is classified as a narrow gauge railway. As I have stated in the introduction, many people regard this gauge only as narrow gauge, but it was this gauge that first gave us these types of railways in this country, so locomotives and stock of this gauge must be included in this book.

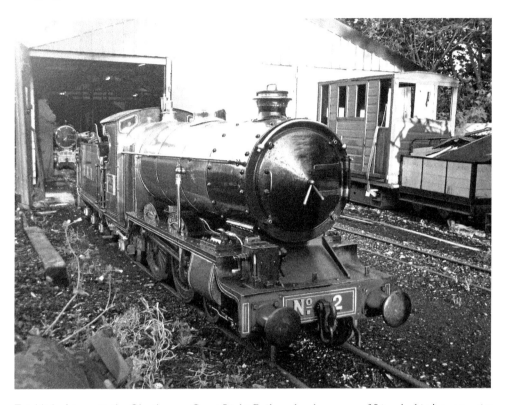

Established in 1948, the Cleethorpes Coast Light Railway has been one of Lincolnshire's top tourist attractions. The railway started out as a 10¼ inch gauge railway, but was re-gauged while under the ownership of the Cleethorpes Borough Council in 1972 to the rather unusual gauge of 14¼ inches. The railway became run down – a lack of money being the reason cited by the Council, which is the same excuse that is usually given by councils who do not wish to continue running something – so it was purchased by a private buyer in the early 1990s, who promptly re-gauged it to its present gauge. In the early part of the twenty-first century the railway was given a National Lottery grant and was able to purchase stock and buildings that had been in storage for almost forty years. This was all part of the Sutton Coldfield Miniature Railway, which had closed in the 1960s, having operated since 1905. One of the locomotives acquired was this lovely looking 4-4-2 locomotive built in 1950, named No. 2 *Sutton Flyer*. It was seen outside of the shed on 26 October 2008.

The main workhorse on the railway is this splendid-looking American-style Sandy River Railroad 2-6-2 locomotive. No. 24 *Sandy River* comes around one of the corners on this 2-mile-long railway on 26 October 2008. This locomotive was built as a 12¼ inch gauge for the Fairbourne Railway in North Wales in 1990. It was re-gauged and came to Cleethorpes in 1997, following trials at the Bure Valley & Kirklees Light Railways. Note how wrapped up the passengers in the train are despite the sun shining in an effort to keep themselves warm on this autumn day on the Lincolnshire coast. The railway is situated in Kings Road, Cleethorpes, DN35 0AG, and further information can be found at www.cclr.co.uk.

In 1975 the popular Cricket St Thomas Wildlife Park, near Chard in Somerset, opened its brand-new attraction in the form of the Cricket St Thomas Railway. The railway formed a 'U' shape around the park and ran for 800 yards. Seen here in its distinctive zebra stripe livery, waiting to depart from the Lemur Wood station on 12 June 2005 was the railway's 1957-built 4w-4w diesel-hydraulic locomotive, named *Saint Thomas*. The Cricket Estate was the setting for the 1970s comedy starring Penelope Keith and Peter Bowles, *To The Manor Born*. It was also the setting for *Noel's House Party* and the infamous Blobbyland – which really finished the park off. Now it is owned by Warner Leisure, offering adult-only luxury breaks. Sadly, the wildlife park and the railway have now all gone, the railway being lifted in 2014.

In 1739 the Dean of Raphoe in County Donegal, in what is now Republic of Ireland, had a deanery named Oakfield Park built, and it was to remain used as such until 1869. Over the years, the house and grounds had been in the ownership of various local families, but had been abandoned and left derelict for many years when they were purchased in 1996 by Sir Gerry and Lady Heather Robinson, who set about the huge task of restoring the house and gardens (which have matured very nicely in the past twenty years, and over 40,000 trees have been planted in the estate). In 2003 the Difflin Lake Railway was built, which winds its way through the trees and gardens on a 2.5-mile journey. On Easter Monday 6 April 2015 the railway's steam locomotive, No. 1 *The Duchess of Difflin*, a 2003 0-4-2T that was built by Exmoor Steam Railway, is seen waiting for its next trainload of passengers to board and begin their ride. The railway also has a 0-4-0 diesel-hydraulic locomotive, which was also running on this very busy day. Further information on the railway and gardens can be found at www.oakfieldpark.com.

Combe Martin in North Devon, EX34 0NG, is the site of the Wildlife & Dinosaur Adventure Park, and within that park the 500-yard-long Earthquake Canyon Railway can be found. The railway opened in 1989 as another attraction to visitors of the park. Seen here on 1 April 2017, in readiness for the first train of the day, is this 1987 Severn Lamb-built 2-8-0 petrol-hydraulic Rio Grande-style steam-outlined locomotive and its two coaches.

As I mentioned in the introduction, in 1896 the then Duke of Westminster commissioned a 15 inch gauge railway to be built on his private Eaton Hall estate in Cheshire. Seen running during one of the occasional public open days held at the Eaton Hall Railway on 4 August 2007 was the railway's resident steam locomotive, the 1994-built 0-4-0T *Katie*.

The Evesham Vale Light Railway was opened in 2002 and winds itself round in a 1,200-yard loop through old orchards and around the 120-acre Evesham Country Park in Worcestershire, WR11 4TP. The railway's oldest locomotive is 4-4-2 No. 32 *Count Louis*, which was built by another of the forefathers of miniature railways in the UK, namely Bassett-Lowke, in 1924. On 29 September 2012, she was seen posing at the head of her train. She is not only the railway's oldest locomotive, but is also the one that does more work than any of the others in any one season. Further details about the Evesham Vale Light Railway can be found at www.evlr.co.uk.

Twinlakes All Action Theme Park in Melton Mowbray, Leicestershire, LE13 1SQ, is the home of two Severn Lamb-built 2-6-0 diesel-hydraulic steam-outlined Rio Grande locomotives. They work the Iron Moose Express Railway that is located within the park grounds. On Bank Holiday Monday 26 August 2013, they were pictured side by side at the furthest end of the railway. The locomotive nearest the camera was built in 1988, and was working the trains that day. The 1986-built locomotive at the rear of the picture was, as you can see by the large wooden sleeper underneath the cow-catcher on the front, out of service on that day. This was due to it suffering a broken wheel a couple of days beforehand. Note the polythene bag wrapped around the driving rod where the wheel should have been.

Clayton West in West Yorkshire, HD8 9XJ, is where the 3.25-mile-long Kirklees Light Railway is situated, 0.25 miles of which is in a tunnel. The railway was opened in October 1991 along the former track bed of a railway that was first proposed to be built through the location in 1846, but was not opened until 1879, and which then ran for just over 103 years until it finally closed in 1983. The railway operates using six locomotives, four of which are steam. This example, *Fox*, pictured in bright sunshine having just run the last working train of the day on 18 July 2012, is a 2-6-2T and is the oldest on the railway, being built by the founder, Brian Taylor, in 1990. There is also a raised dual-gauge (5 inch and 7¼ inch) line at this location. Visit ww.kirkleeslightrailway.com for further details.

Marwell's Wonderful Railway is one of the many attractions that can be found at the 140 acre site that makes up the Marwell Zoo in Hampshire, SO21 1JH (www.marwell.org.uk). The fifteen to twenty-minute journey on the 900-yard track takes passengers close to the animal enclosures and provides some real opportunities to get close-up views of some of the endangered species found at the zoo. The railway and its four coaches (which can carry sixty-four passengers at one time) are operated by this 1987 Severn Lamb-built 2-6-0 diesel-hydraulic steam-outlined engine, *Princess Anne,* which was seen in between trains on 2 October 2011.

Located in Cumbria, CA18 1SW, the Ravenglass & Eskdale Railway is one of the oldest miniature railways in the country. The original line was built in 1873 as a 3 foot gauge and was commercially opened in May 1875 to convey iron ore to Ravenglass, where it was transferred onto the main line and taken to Barrow-in-Furness. The first passenger trains would start a year later, in 1876. The line was closed in 1913 due to the diminishing amount of iron ore being transported. In 1915 W. J. Bassett-Lowke and R. Proctor-Mitchell acquired the line to test their locomotives on and promptly began re-gauging it to the size it is today. The railway was put up for sale in 1958 and things looked bleak. However, in 1960 the Ravenglass & Eskdale Railway Preservation Society was formed, and with the help of a wealthy stockbroker and a local landowner, they purchased the railway for the sum of £12,000. The railway now runs for 7 miles across the glorious and often rugged Cumbrian countryside and the journey takes about forty minutes. The railway has an assortment of rolling stock and about twenty locomotives, more or less evenly matched between steam and diesel/petrol. The oldest locomotive on the railway is this 0-8-2 locomotive, No. 3 *River Irt,* which was built in 1894. It is seen here on 19 July 2015 inside the workshop shed. The covers are put onto the boiler on miniature steam locomotives in order to assist with its cooling down after they have been running trains all day. A further in-depth history and information on the railway can be found at www.ravenglass-railway.co.uk.

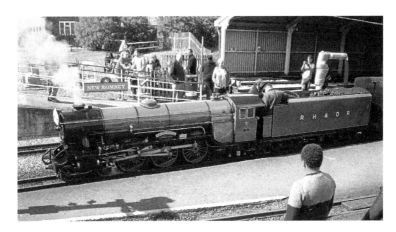

The Romney, Hythe & Dymchurch Railway is probably one of the best known miniature railways in the UK, running for 14 miles between Hythe and Dungeness (famous for its power station and numerous houses made out of old railway carriages). The railway was the culmination of two gentlemen, namely Captain J. E. P Howey and Count Louis Zborowski. The former was an ex-Army officer, a millionaire landowner and a knowledgeable man when it came to miniature railways, while the latter was well known for being a racing driver and was regarded as being considerably richer than the former. Between them they tried and failed to purchase the Ravenglass & Eskdale Railway in Cumbria, so they decided to build their own, and Kent was suggested and decided upon. In 1927 the railway was officially opened, although the double track only covered the 8 miles between Romney & New Hythe. However, the following year the twin track line had reached Dungeness, giving the railway a distance of an impressive 13.5 miles. The railway has an impressive fleet of eleven steam locomotives, two passenger diesels and three locos used for permanent way work. They also have over sixty passenger coaches alone, including a 'bar-car', which is the longest vehicle that has been built to run on lines of this gauge. Designed by Henry Greenly and built by Davey-Paxman & Company in Colchester, Essex, this 1925 4-6-2 locomotive, No. 1 *Green Goddess*, was the first locomotive that was built for the railway. On 18 April 2014 she was getting up steam and preparing to depart New Romney station (TN28 8PL), which is the railway's main base and where all of its rolling stock, sheds and workshops are located. For more information visit their website at www.rhdr.org.uk.

Two steam locomotives that previously ran on a private railway in Gloucestershire now offer regular steam power on the Sherwood Forest Railway in Edwinstowe, Nottinghamshire, NG21 9HL, giving a 1-mile ride through cuttings and across traditional farmland. The two locomotives in question are Nos 1 *Smokey Joe* and 2 *Pet*. Both are 0-4-0ST+T locomotives and were built in 1991 and 1998 respectively. They are seen at the further end of the line after double heading their train prior to making the return trip on 26 August 2013.

Located within an amusement park on the seafront in Tramore, County Waterford, Ireland, is the 400-yard circular Tramore Miniature Railway. Opened in 1973 the line passes through two tunnels, which have locking doors at either end and are used as sheds to store the locomotive and rolling stock in when the railway is closed. During the height of the season the railway often continues to operate well into the summer evenings. The motive power is provided by the 1973-built Severn Lamb Rio Grande 2-8-0 steam-outlined petrol-hydraulic locomotive and the coaches are four of the four-compartment ride-in roofed bogie type. On 28 April 2011 the loco was taken out of the sheds by the operator to allow myself and three good friends the opportunity to photograph it. The operator also treated us to a ride around the circuit; it was not a normal running day and he was on-site carrying out work in preparation for the start of the operating season in May.

I have referred many times to the four-compartment ride-in roofed bogie carriage as being the more usual type found on railways of this gauge. Pictured on 16 April 2017 at the Westport House & Childrens Zoo in County Mayo are an example of what these coaches look like. Here, No. 3F and two other coaches that are used on the 700-yard-long Westport House Express wait patiently while the 1989 Severn Lamb Rio Grande steam-outlined 2-6-0 diesel-hydraulic *W. H.* runs around to the front of the stock. Note that no passengers are permitted onto the carriages until the locomotive is attached to the front of the train.

Located at Red Cat Lane in Burscough, Lancashire, L40 1UQ, is the Windmill Animal Farm and its miniature 1-mile-long railway (www.windmillanimalfarm.co.uk). Pictured here on 27 August 2008, and looking rather large and imposing as it takes on water ahead of the day's running, is the 2001-built Exmoor Steam Railway 2-6-2T *St Christopher*.

In the Buckinghamshire countryside, not far from Aylesbury, is the privately run Wotton Light Railway, which comprises three locomotives and four coaches. One of those locomotives is this 1996-built Exmoor Steam Railway 0-6-0T, *Sandy*, which was pictured in steam and ready to run the first train of the day on a specially arranged visit to the railway on 15 August 2010.

The railway, as I have mentioned, has four coaches. One of those is a totally enclosed bogie open-plan saloon, and the others comprise three two-compartment ride-in roofed bogie types. This particular example has been fitted by the owner with two small round tables, which makes a unique coach where miniature railways are concerned.

Chapter 13 – Portable and Non-Permanent Lines

Although the majority of railways (of all gauges contained within this book) are permanent locations, there are also a reasonable number of portable railways, which are taken to a location, such as an event, where the track, locomotives and stock are set up and are then removed again at the end of said event. In this chapter I will look at some of these types of railways.

I mentioned previously that the 7¼ Inch Gauge Society held their AGM on 11 October 2014 at the Bath & West Railway in Shepton Mallet. Although this railway is a permanent one, in order to be able to run on the line a portable track needed to be laid from the large shed which was used as a makeshift turntable and storage site at a part of the running line where the two would be joined. Pictured on that day was this unusual vertical-boilered steam railcar, No. 7 *The Sentinel*, as it emerged from the shed and made its way slowly to the running lines. Note that the rails are not the usual shape, but are merely lengths of flat metal that rest in wooden blocks with grooves cut into them.

On 13 September 2014 the Moseley Railway Trust held a 'Tracks to the Trenches' event at their base within the grounds of the Apedale Heritage Centre & Community Park in Chesterton, Staffordshire. The event was to commemorate the 100th anniversary of the start of the First World War, and it featured many locomotives and rolling stock from the time, as well as road vehicles, steam traction engines and a replica Mk IV tank. There was also a portable 7¼ inch gauge railway and one of the two locomotives present was this recently built 4w petrol-electric scale model of an armoured-type Simplex bread bin locomotive, No. 2785. Note that the rails are standard shape, and how the track is propped up to keep it stable with long, white, durable plastic strips that have been placed under the sleepers.

Every year at Tarrant Hinton, in Dorset, hundreds of thousands attend the world-famous annual five-day Great Dorset Steam Fair. In 2009 there were four portable railways at this event, using two steam and two diesel-hydraulic locomotives from the closed (2006) Dobwalls Family Adventure American Theme Park Miniature Railway near Liskeard, in Cornwall. This picture of a David Curwen-built 1980 2-8-2 Rio Grande Railway locomotive, No. 498 *Otto Mears*, was taken on 5 September 2009. As can be seen from the picture, even on miniature railways people prefer to travel behind a steam locomotive, as the train is well packed and the diesel train behind it is empty – and that was how it was for the majority of the five days of the event. Worth noting is that all of the locomotives from this railway are now in Australia, the majority going to the Diamond Valley Railway in Eltham, which is a suburb of Melbourne, except for one, which can be seen at the Eastleigh Lakeside Railway in Hampshire.

Another portable railway was seen at the South West Trains, Siemens Transport Northam depot in Hampshire during the open day held there on 12 October 2013. In charge of the trains on that day was this 2012-built 0-6-0T locomotive, No. 684 *Wensleydale*, from the Great Cockrow Railway in Chertsey, Surrey. Note how the track has been stabilised by fixing it to long planks of wood, because if the sleepers were placed directly onto the surface of the car park it would become unsteady during the course of the day.

The West Somerset Railway Association hold a yearly Steam Fayre & Vintage Vehicle Show at their site in Norton Fitzwarren, just outside of Taunton. This event usually takes place on the first weekend in August. Pictured on 6 August 2011 was this 1996-built 2-4-2T engine, No. 3 *Tinkerbell*, as it poses on the portable track in front on the standard gauge freight wagons from the West Somerset Railway that are on display.

Chapter 14 – Static Exhibits

Many miniature railway locomotives tend to end up inside museums, and are usually displayed inside of glass cases, although this is not always the case, as I have detailed previously. In this chapter I shall look at more of these exhibits, some of them having some rather bizarre and out of the ordinary gauges. Not all of them were ever built as working locomotives, but rather just as models.

At first glance you could be forgiven if you thought that this model was indeed a miniature locomotive. In fact, this splendid and detailed 1983-built 4-4-0, No. 736, is actually only 10¼ inch gauge. It was pictured on 3 June 2012 inside the museum during an open day at the privately owned Sir William McAlpine Fawley Hill Railway, located in Buckinghamshire.

Among its collection on display, the Head of Steam Museum in Darlington has three standard gauge locomotives that were all built in the nineteenth century, and this unusual 11¾ inch gauge 2-2-2 non-working model locomotive, No. 1, which was built *c.* 1848. Photographed on 18 October 2014, it must be pointed out that the museum has made a fundamental error regarding this model, in that they have decided to display it on the floor of the building, and even on scale models of this size this can damage the rail wheels, often beyond repair, if stored off track for long periods of time.

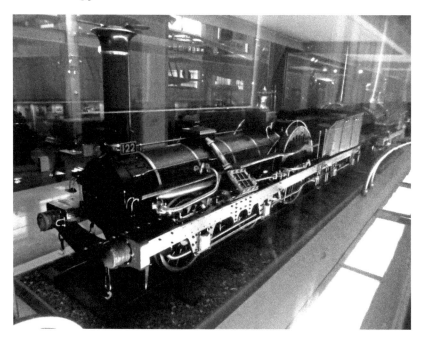

The Science Museum in the London borough of South Kensington has numerous miniature railway locomotives on display in glass cases. Pictured on 19 May 2012 is this 2-2-2-0 locomotive, No. 122 *Jeanne D'Arc*, which was built around 1851 and is 8¾ inch gauge.

One location that has in the region of approximately fifty miniature locomotives on display is the National Railway Museum in York. The majority of these are located within 'The Warehouse' in glass cases that are stacked above head height, lining the walls and in the centre of the building. There are some models that can be found in the main hall, dotted around the edges, and one of these is this 7¼ inch scale model of a Great Western Railway King Class 4-6-0. Built around 1939, No. 6000 *King George V* was pictured keeping company with headboards, nameplates and other railway artefacts on 7 April 2012.

The McGarigle Machine Co. of Niagara Falls in Buffalo, New York, was where the uncle of the four Cagney brothers, Peter McGarigle, built the Cagney locomotives that would be exported to Britain and other countries. Located inside of the Strumpshaw Hall Steam Museum in Acle, Norfolk, is where this particular 4-4-0 Cagney locomotive can be seen. No. 2 *Brooks Railroad* was built in 1902 and is of 15 inch gauge. It was pictured on 12 August 2007. Note that just visible behind it is the front of a *c.* 1963 Triang-built Golden Arrow 10¼ inch gauge battery-electric locomotive.

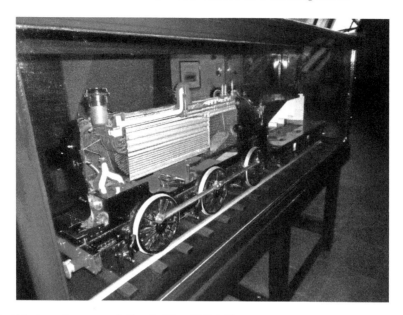

Located within the main transport hall at the Ulster Folk & Transport Museum in Cultra, Belfast, among the many exhibits of locomotives and rolling stock, is this scale model which is an 8 inch gauge of an unidentified 0-6-0T locomotive that has been sectioned to show what the inside of a steam locomotive looks like. It was pictured on 4 April 2015.

Sandy Bay near Exmouth in Devon has the World of Country Life as one of its major tourist attractions. There are farm animals, deer, children's play areas, falconry displays and several transport-related exhibits. There are three items of railway interest: two are static exhibits of 18 inch gauge steam locomotives, which are outside of the scope of this book, and there is also this 7¼ inch gauge 4w-4w petrol-hydraulic locomotive, No. 300, which is based on the Amtrak EMD F40PH locomotives that were built between 1975 and 1998. This locomotive has been donated to the museum by the owner as it was the locomotive that was used on the miniature railway that operated here for some time during the 1980s and 1990s. It was pictured as a static exhibit in front of a Trabant motor car when photographed on 14 September 2014.